Be My People

Be My People

Sermons on the Ten Commandments

Ross W. Marrs

Abingdon Press
Nashville

BE MY PEOPLE: SERMONS ON THE TEN COMMANDMENTS

Copyright © 1991 by Abingdon Press

This book is printed on recycled, acid-free paper.

Library of Congress Cataloging-in-Publication Data

Marrs, Ross W., 1926-
    Be my people : sermons on the Ten Commandments / Ross W. Marrs.
        p.   cm. – (The Protestant pulpit exchange)
    Includes bibliographical references.
    ISBN 0-687-02826-4 (alk. paper)
    1.   Ten Commandments–Sermons.   2. Sermons, American.   I. Title.
II. Series.
BV4655.M26   1991   90-26298
241.5'2–dc20   CIP

Scripture quotations, unless otherwise indicated, are from the
New Revised Standard Version Bible, copyright © 1989, by the Division of
Christian Education of the National Council of the Churches of Christ in the
United States of America.

Those noted KJV are from the King James Version of the Bible.

The excerpt from "Choruses From the Rock," on p. 45, by T.S. Eliot is From
COLLECTED POEMS 1909–1962. Copyright © 1936 by Harcourt Brace
Jovanovich, Inc., copyright 1963, 1964 by T.S. Eliot. Reprinted by permission
of Harcourt Brace Jovanovich, Inc., and Faber and Faber Limited.

MANUFACTURED IN THE UNITED STATES OF AMERICA

To my wife,
Jean,
with appreciation

Contents

Preface

After forty years of striving to be an effective communicator of the good news of Jesus Christ, I have learned that those who think that sermon preparation is easy or begins on the Friday before Sunday have never accorded the discipline of preaching the attention and honor it deserves. To be granted the opportunity to struggle with life's issues, faith questions, and our ever-changing existence is a great privilege. To have faithful, searching people come and listen is to be paid the highest compliment.

For me the sermon ought first of all to be scriptural. That does not mean that we write down our thoughts for the day and then seek to bolster them with quotations from the Bible. Rather, it means that we do our homework, that we fully investigate the scriptures and ask the questions, "Who wrote it?" "When was it written?" "To whom was it addressed?" and "What was its original message?" Only when we have thoroughly investigated these matters and availed ourselves of the latest scholarship in biblical studies, history, theology, philosophy, psychology, and the like are we given the freedom to apply what we have discovered to contemporary life.

The reader will not be required to read far into this book to discover that I like to use illustrations from life to shed light here and there. Dr. Clovis Chappel, a great communicator-preacher from the first half of this century once said to me, "No one has lived a life so void of experience that living illustrations cannot be gleaned from it. Such illustrations are more authentic and have the ring of life about them." The serious practitioner of the art of preaching ought to:

9

1. *Visit.* Know your congregation. Know their values, life-style, employment, presuppositions, concerns, and commitment.

2. *Build a library.* Ordinary books are of little value. Reference books, commentaries, theologies, philosophies, books focused on preaching skills, and the like are a must.

3. *Plan ahead.* Working from week to week produces only shallow observations. Planning sermons well in advance enables one to gather material from life experiences, reading, and encounters, and allows one to be alert and to listen for meaningful input, to be open to life itself.

4. *Read everything in sight*—books, newspapers, magazines, professional journals, and the like. One can never find time to read everything, but a good preacher is a faithful reader.

5. *Write all the time.* Write about everything. Practice the arts of illustration, punctuation, clarity, and effective communication.

6. *Teach no less than one class each week.* Do in-depth Bible study with your lay members, and you will learn more than they. Project your preaching a year or two in advance as to themes and then teach the material ahead of time. Then much of your sermon preparation will be done.

7. *Be disciplined.* I have no formulas or easy patterns for success. Each person must discover what works best, and once that is known stick with it, nurture it, and practice it.

8. *Use series.* If you consider the church year, know the needs of the congregation, and have been teaching, reading, and planning ahead, you will find that a series of four to eight sermons will provide continuity for the hearers that will be more valuable than jumping from one text to another from week to week.

9. *Be open to the Holy Spirit.* Begin in the study. If you do not hear the voice of the Spirit in the study, you will in all likelihood not hear it in the pulpit. Being open to the voice of God, urging, correcting, challenging, directing, and providing insight is essential.

10. *Listen with ears and eyes as you preach and afterward.* What most have to say to the preacher at the back of the sanctuary is just filler spoken for the want of something meaning-

ful to say. You will learn who to listen to and what to hear.
Then take it seriously and let it affect your preaching.

I thank each of the congregations that have allowed me the
privilege of practicing on them. I am grateful for their kind
and helpful observations. A special word is due to my wife,
Jean, who both encourages excellence and makes room for
its pursuit. And I am grateful to my colleagues: Don Winslow,
a valued lay friend; John Thomas, my associate; and Dr.
Leonard Sweet, President of United Theological Seminary in
Dayton, Ohio, who have read, reflected, and made cogent
and valued suggestions.

It is my hope that these sermons will not only provide
insight and shed light on the subject at hand, but that they
might also serve as illustrations of my convictions about the
cherished gift of preaching.

Ross W. Marrs

Introduction

I grew up in a southern West Virginia coal mining town and attended a community church that worshiped in a one-room building. Sunday school classes were held in cubicles marked off by a cloth hung on wires. On the wall next to the cubicle reserved for my class hung a large 3-by-6-foot chart (it seemed larger) on which was printed the Ten Commandments in the King James Version, similar to what follows.

1. Thou shalt have no other gods before me.
2. Thou shalt not make unto thee any graven image.
3. Thou shalt not take the name of the Lord thy God in vain.
4. Remember the sabbath day, to keep it holy.
5. Honour thy father and thy mother.
6. Thou shalt not kill.
7. Thou shalt not commit adultery.
8. Thou shalt not steal.
9. Thou shalt not bear false witness.
10. Thou shalt not covet.

There that chart hung, week after week, month after month, year after year; its silent witness threatening anyone who dared violate its commands. The very presence of this poster seemed to imply that if you kept all these commands you could surely count on God's approval. If you kept nine and broke just one, you surely were damned to hell.

I have a suspicion that there are many persons who still carry such a chart about in their minds and that they carry something of this attitude toward what we call the Ten Commandments.

Many of us are convinced that the commandments must be important because they are in the Bible, that in some way these words do relate to our lives, even though we are not sure just how. So the words are honored more by our attitudes than by our keeping them.

Surely now is a proper time for us to take a fresh look at this sacred document, which is better called "the ten words." The experiences of this century have revealed us to be a people awash in a quagmire of immorality. Stories of infidelity, betrayal, abandonment, disloyalty, illegality, assassination, embezzlement, law breaking, lying, cheating, rampant self-indulgence, influence peddling, addiction, murder, and the like are spread before us in the media daily.

On every hand, voices call for a return of morality, adoption of new codes of ethics, and training in character development, designed to lead us back to national sanity and safety.

Now, as never before, it is time to talk about the Ten Commandments and to ask whether they have anything to say to us in the twentieth century. If we are to hear the messages that can be relevant to us in these words, we had better begin by reminding ourselves of the story that lies behind them.

The Story

That story begins, as reported in Genesis 12, with a call for a man named Abram to leave his country and kin and to follow the voice that promised a new land and a great heritage. Most of us have traced the story of the trek to Canaan, and we know about Isaac and Jacob and Joseph. We have heard the story of the famine that brought Joseph's people to Egypt and how the new rulers of Egypt, who were actually the old rulers, had placed them in bondage. The Hyksos, who had earlier swept victoriously through that entire region and dominated for many decades, had been overcome by the Egyptians, who once again began to rule their own affairs. It is they who do not know Joseph and place the Hebrew people in bondage (see Exod. 18).

Most of us are well informed about the great Exodus and God's rescue of his people. As children we were enthralled by stories of the baby Moses in a basket, the man Moses at the burning bush and engaged in a contest with the magicians of Egypt. We were appalled by the great plagues that tormented the Egyptians, held in awe at the final plague that brought so much death, and thrilled at the escape, the rolling back of the waters for the escapees and the drowning of their pursuers. Like many others, we plodded through the wilderness with Moses and his unwilling people until God brought them to a special place. We read:

> On the third new moon after the Israelites had gone out of the land of Egypt, on that very day, they came into the wilderness of Sinai. They had journeyed from Rephidim, entered the wilderness of Sinai, and camped in the wilderness; Israel camped there in front of the mountain. Then Moses went up to God; the LORD called to him from the mountain, saying, "Thus you shall say to the house of Jacob, and tell the Israelites: You have seen what I did to the Egyptians, and how I bore you on eagles' wings and brought you to myself. Now therefore, if you obey my voice and keep my covenant, you shall be my treasured possession out of all the peoples. Indeed, the whole earth is mine, but you shall be for me a priestly kingdom and a holy nation." (Exod. 19:1-6)

Standing in fear and awe at the foot of the mountain, the recently freed slaves are treated to a display of the power and might of God. It is there, we are told, that they are given the law, which includes the Ten Commandments, or the ten words (or messages), of God.

15

Intent

It is God who takes initiative and comes to make them God's people. Out of sheer undeserved divine grace, God has chosen a nameless band of worthless slaves to be God's own. The writer of Deuteronomy reminded them later:

> You are a people holy to the LORD your God; the LORD your God has chosen you out of all the peoples on earth to be his people, his treasured possession. It was not because you were more numerous than any other people that the LORD set his heart on you and chose you—for you were the fewest of all peoples. (Deut. 7:6-7)

This same message is repeated in Deuteronomy 9 with the reminder that "It is not because of your righteousness or the uprightness of your heart that you are going in to occupy [the] land" (Deut. 9:5*a*). These commandments are not rules the people must keep in order to be acceptable and worthy of being chosen by God. They are already chosen, and not because of any merit of their own. God's covenant is already made with them; keeping the commandments is to be their obedience, their response for what God already has done.

This is a band of slaves, unorganized, untrained, unprepared for what lies before them. It is clear that this God intends to lead them as a people to a land and there make them into a new nation that is to accomplish God's purposes for them.

These instructions are not so much rules, which each individual must keep, as they are words, God's messages, a spelling out of the basis for the creation of a new community, a design for the making of a nation. In these words the new community will find its life, base its unity, and discover a place for anchoring its life. Here it would come to possess that commitment and spirit that would enable it to truly be the people of God.

Structure

One could maintain that if the material in Exodus was edited into the Torah during the Babylonian exile, the purpose of these words is better fitted to the needs of that new community that Ezra and Nehemiah were to establish after the exile. One could argue that these commandments (words) could prove useful at both occasions.

In either case, it is my contention that rather than ten separate moral commands to be kept by individuals forever, as proof of being worthy of God's love, these words presented here are the four essential bases for community. Consider this outline (based on the New Revised Standard Version).

A. God.
  1. You shall have no other gods before me.
  2. You shall not make for yourself an idol.
  3. You shall not make wrongful use of the name of the Lord your God.
B. The Individual
  4. Remember the sabbath day, and keep it holy.
C. The Family
  5. Honor your father and your mother.
D. Society
  6. You shall not murder.
  7. You shall not commit adultery.
  8. You shall not steal.
  9. You shall not bear false witness.
  10. You shall not covet.

The first three commandments are a proper response to a gracious God. The fourth (the one about the sabbath) is not, as some suppose, a word about God, but a word about ourselves, as we shall see. The fifth addresses the need to protect and nurture the family. The sixth through the tenth speak to major concerns that lie at the base of social relationships: God, self, family, and others; the four essential bases of community.

Therefore, in these sermons I will consider the commandments one by one, but all the while keep in mind the basic premise that these instructions are not ten moral commandments, but ten words (messages) comprising four basic principles on which a new community is to be based. Where applicable, I will refer to the exodus and the exile stories and seek to show how these words held meaning for the people undergoing widely differing experiences. Above all else, I mean to help us, in the twentieth century, stand alongside those recently freed slaves at Sinai, and will show how we still keep company with those exiles leaving Babylon for the home of their ancestors. If we are to benefit from these words, it will be because we too stand in the presence of a God who has chosen us when we did not deserve to be chosen.

THE FIRST WORD

> *I am the LORD your God, who brought you
> out of the land of Egypt, out of the house of
> slavery; you shall have no other gods before me.*
> *(Exod. 20:2-3)*

The Choosy God

Any consideration of the first or all of the Ten Commandments must begin with this prologue, this reminder that there is one who has taken initiative to bring a people out of bondage. The Exodus writer recalls the event:

> The Israelites groaned under their slavery, and cried out. Out of slavery their cry for help rose up to God. God heard their groaning, and God remembered his covenant with Abraham, Isaac, and Jacob. God looked upon the Israelites, and God took notice of them. (Exod. 2:23*b*-25)

All too many imagine the God we meet in the Hebrew scriptures to be a God of wrath and judgment. The prologue to the Ten Commandments says otherwise. We take the commandments seriously, not because we are afraid not to or because we will go to hell if we do not, but because they are a proper response to a God who makes us God's own even when we have not deserved it. Surely those rag-tag slaves in Egypt, who had been buried in slavery perhaps more than four hundred years (see Exod. 12:40), had nothing to offer God. The Egyptians had reclaimed the throne for their Pharaoh in 1580 BCE (see Exod. 1:8), and it is probable that the Pharaoh who enslaved them was Rameses II, who ruled Egypt from 1291 to 1225 BCE. (See Elmer W. K. Mould,

Essentials of Bible History [New York: Ronald Press, 1951], p. 96.)

> *"God . . . makes us God's own even when we have not deserved it."*

God's coming to them was a story of sheer grace. Once no people, now they are made God's people. This initiative and claim by God requires obedience as their response to sheer grace. As Christians, we have heard the same word. Paul put it down for us in his letter to the Romans: "God proves his love for us in that while we still were sinners Christ died for us" (Rom. 5:8).

This is the God who has come to a worthless people, who do not even know who he is, and has taken great risks on their behalf. The preachers of Israel remind the people that this God has made them in his image (Gen. 1:26), has given them dominion (Gen. 1:26*b*), and has given them his name (Exod. 3:13-15).

"You shall have no other gods before me" (Exod. 20:3). If the recently freed slaves who stand at the foot of Mount Sinai are the first to hear these words, it seems clear that for them this is no call to monotheism. Here we encounter henotheism, the claim that Israel's God is to be regarded as first above all other gods. It is an admonition that (if there are other gods) this God, I AM, Yahweh, the God of Abraham, Isaac and Jacob, is to be their God. Yahweh has taken possession of these people, and they are to obey the commands.

If, however, these words were penned into the story of Israel when the Torah was fashioned in Babylon, the first word is a call to monotheism. One only has to read the record of the kings of Israel and Judah to learn that they were a mixed lot so far as faithfulness to Yahweh was concerned. Many of them, Ahab the worst, led the people into the worship of foreign gods. The writer of II Kings summarizes the situation at the time of the Assyrian exile of the northern tribes and says of the people: "They worshiped the LORD but also served their own gods" (II Kings 17:33).

Exile in Babylon forever cured the Israelites of their "awhoring after other gods"; ever since, they have been incurably monotheistic. When Ezra and Nehemiah bring the people back home, it is for the purpose of establishing a single-hearted people on the basis of religious purity. "You shall be holy, for I the LORD your God am holy" (Lev. 19:2*b*).

It does not matter to which time you assign these words because in Israel the people saw themselves as sharing the experiences of those who had come before them. If God had addressed their ancestors, they too had been addressed. If their ancestors had undergone an experience, that experience was also theirs. Listen to the pronouns in the creedal form of the response that the people are commanded to make when they come into their new land: "The Egyptians treated *us* harshly and afflicted *us,* by imposing hard labor on *us, we* cried to the LORD, the God of *our* ancestors; the LORD heard *our* voice and saw *our* affliction, *our* toil, and *our* oppression" (Deut. 26:6-7, italics added).

There are those among us who imagine this command to have been proper for a primitive and superstitious people of long ago. We have heard that they lived among a people who worshiped many gods. They saw the splendor and majesty of Egypt and were impressed with their gods. They saw the success of those who worshiped the baals when they came to Canaan and were convinced that these nature gods could assure agricultural success. They were no doubt influenced by the worship of the golden calf that was current among the Canaanites. They were dazzled by the processionals of the worshipers of Marduk in Babylon; some converted and never looked back.

> ## *"All the old gods still prowl among us and win our favor."*

We can understand their temptations. But us? We are monotheists, and this is not our problem. Perhaps we need to take another look at ourselves. Just a cursory glimpse will reveal that all the old gods still prowl among us and win our favor. One does not identify the gods of a people by those they call by name but by those they serve. Who would deny that we are a people who bow at other altars, that, like the people of the eighth century BCE, we too fear the Lord and worship our own gods?

The baals of Canaan, fertility gods of the past, still claim their devotees in those who revere sex and intercourse as the pivotal forces in life. Who can watch television for more than a moment and not be confronted by some modern baal promising youth and beauty and the gift of a life force and virility that will make us admired by all?

Who would deny that we are a people who have listened to the promises of the god Mars, god of war. We pour out our treasure, and then lay the lives of our young upon the altar of Mars. We build machines of destruction and name them with peaceful names—and we know all the time that, while we may escape war, we may fall victim to a depletion of our resources brought on by our fears, anxieties, and greed. When someone suggests that we can close a military base, not build one more submarine, let one rocket go unfinished, mark off one squadron of planes, we are reminded that even though we do not need them for war, we need them to keep the wheels of our economic system turning. What promised peace has, instead, become a bondage.

Whether taken from a bottle or as a pill or in a snort of powder, many still seek the comforts, reassurances, and thrills promised by Bacchus, god of the vine. On the one hand, there are those in our society who struggle to reveal the fabric of individual lives and of society torn asunder by the addictions that ravage and destroy, while on the other hand both government and business encourage this worship because of the income it generates.

Mammon reigns supreme in a society that truly does believe that meaning and worth are to be had through many possessions.

Venus and Cupid lurk in every corner and on every street by convincing many that romantic love will last and that when we are "in love" we are ready for marriage.

Minerva dangles the temptation to believe that our own intelligence and wisdom are enough for us and that we no longer need God, that we have come away from superstitious times and now are enlightened and can make life on our own. Who would not say that we are like those of Israel of long ago, who "feared the Lord but also served their own gods." Jesus' commentary on the first commandment is a reminder that those who chase after all the gods cannot be a people of unity, wholeness (shalom), and peace. He said that, "No one can serve two masters; for a slave will either hate the one and love the other, or be devoted the one and despise the other. You cannot serve God and wealth" (Matt. 6:24).

The message to the slaves who stood at the foot of Mount Sinai was clear. God had taken initiative to free them from bondage and had brought them to this place to make a covenant with them. Yahweh was to be their (only) God, and they were to be God's people. Their response was obedience.

The message to those who followed Ezra and Nehemiah back to Jerusalem was the same. It was God who had come to bring them home.

The prophet Isaiah had declared it:

> Comfort, O comfort my people,
>   says your God.
> Speak tenderly to Jerusalem,
>   and cry to her

that she has served her term,
  that her penalty is paid,
that she has received from the
    Lord's hand
  double for all her sins.

A voice cries out:
"In the wilderness prepared the
    way of the Lord,
  make straight in the desert a
    highway for our God. . . .
Then the glory of the Lord shall
    be revealed,
  and all people shall see it
    together,
  for the mouth of the Lord has
    spoken. (Isa. 40:1-3, 5)

When Jesus is asked to name the first and greatest commandment he will have a ready response, garnered from knowledge of the scriptures of Israel: "Hear, O Israel: the Lord our
God, the Lord is one; you shall love the Lord your God with
all your heart, and with all your soul, and with all your mind,
and with all your strength" (Mark 12:29-30). The message in
our own day is as clear now as it was then. If we are to have
community, if we are to have peace with one another, we
must begin with single-hearted allegiance and loyalty to the
God who has claimed us.

In Christ, God has taken the initiative for our time. This is
the God, Matthew writes, who is Immanuel, God with us.
God's pursuit of us continues as it has continued through the
ages. The God who came to Eden and asked of the first man
and woman, "Where are you?" is the same God who comes in
Christ at the end of the scriptures and invites: "Listen! I am
standing at the door, knocking; if you hear my voice and
open the door, I will come in to you and eat with you, and
you with me" (Rev. 3:20).

24

> *"Wherever a people bow at no altar or at many altars and call upon the names of many gods, there can be no unity and no community."*

Wherever a people bow at no altar or at many altars and call upon the names of many gods, there can be no unity and no community. What they value, their view of life, their attitudes toward one another, their allegiances, that for which they will sacrifice will be shaped by their concept of the god(s) they worship. Like a giant social centrifuge, the whirling winds of multiple faiths will tear the fabric of the nation asunder.

In any nation in which many declare that no gods are needed, there is no central place of allegiance to bind the people into one.

In a nation where the name of God is mouthed faithfully at church by a people who pay homage at many other altars all week, we ought not to be surprised at the moral and personal dilemmas that afflict us.

In a nation that considers itself Christian but is fascinated with the power of the gods of other nations, there ought not to be surprise at our lack of national goals and direction.

You shall have no other gods before me. Whether this command declares that Yahweh is first among all the gods, or whether it means that Yahweh alone is god, the meaning is the same. There is one who comes to us in our darkest moments and delivers us and then lays claim to us and our obedience.

That obedience is not demanded just so that we measure up to some arbitrary rules meant just to see if we can make it, but because in obedience life is found. Those who hear this word and do it are made whole. Those who seek God's will above all else gain the gift of shalom, peace, wholeness.

The prophet Isaiah spoke a needed word for his people as they faced exile to Babylon. That word still stands as God's word to all the nations at any time:

> Thus says the LORD, the King of Israel,
>   and his Redeemer, the LORD of hosts:
> I am the first and I am the last;
>   besides me there is no god. (Isa. 44:6)

THE SECOND WORD

> *You shall not make for yourself an idol, whether in the form of anything that is heaven above, or that is on the earth beneath, or that is in the water under the earth. You shall not bow down to them or worship them; for I the LORD your God am a jealous God, punishing children for the iniquity of parents, to the third and the fourth generation of those who reject me, but showing steadfast love to the thousandth generation of those who love me and keep my commandments. (Exod. 20:4-6)*

The Jealous God

*I*magine the scene when the commandments were first given. Here, according to the biblical story, is a motley group of rag-tag slaves recently freed from Egyptian bondage, standing at the foot of a smoking mountain, ears ringing from loud trumpet blasts, shaken by the trembling earth, and hearing the command: "You shall not make for yourself an idol." I will never forget those scenes in the movie *The Ten Commandments,* in which Charlton Heston, as Moses, covers his face while God blasts the words of the commands (in Hebrew), onto the tablets of stone. You can imagine the fright of the people standing at the foot of that mountain.

One is likely to conclude that these people would know very little about idols, but such is not the case. Take time to review the story of their ancestors, and you will soon come upon the story of Jacob and Laban and their argument over Jacob's wanting to strike out on his own. Just as a precaution,

Rachel, daughter of Laban, filches her father's household gods while he is away, and she and Jacob begin their run for freedom. Biblical writers always like to poke fun at idols, and they do a good job of it here. When Laban catches up with the two refugees, he is more interested in recovering his idols than anything else and wants to search the caravan. Rachel has hidden them under her saddle and pleads "the way of women" as her reason for not wanting to dismount. Laban is bilked, but best of all the idol is shown as not even having the power to cry out for help.

They had seen idols in Egypt, too. Brilliant representations of the sun god Ra must have impressed them. That they remember the idols of Egypt is recorded in the story of their impatience with Moses, who has climbed the mountain to talk to that invisible God. They convince Aaron, brother of Moses, to make them a golden calf and throw a great festival for the occasion. It must have been some party, because the noise caught God's attention.

If you are a historian and wish to claim that these commands were for those who were leaving Babylon and returning home to establish a holy community, the case is the same. The exiles also knew about idols. They had stood and watched the splendor of the processionals of Marduk in Babylon, and they would get the message, too.

To such as these, and to all since, the command has stood clear: "You shall not make for yourself an idol."

Why?

Why would such a thing matter to one who was really God? Weren't all those other people able to better conceive their gods when they had images handy? Wouldn't that make God more real for them?

> *"When idols are made, the Creator is blended with creation."*

Part of the answer is contained in the command itself: "I the LORD your God am a jealous God" (Exod. 20:5*b*). The case against idols is even stronger in an older source. In Deuteronomy 27:15 we read: "Cursed be anyone who makes an idol or casts an image, anything abhorrent to the LORD, the work of an artisan, and sets it up in secret."

Idols are abhorrent to God, and God is jealous because when idols are made, the Creator is blended with creation. A constant theme of the Hebrew scriptures maintains that Yahweh is not to be identified with nature; it is Yahweh who created all things, sustains all things, and provides a future for all things. Other cultures with whom Israel came in contact identified the powers of the universe as gods, gave their worship to the baals, lords of the land, that represented the powers of nature. That worship was designed to placate and influence the gods so that they would shower their blessings on the people.

Yahweh showers blessings on God's people without being asked. God's bounty is given to all, the deserving and the undeserving. To confuse God with nature is to erase the divine fingerprint from creation and reduce the creator to a lesser functioning power.

Everywhere one turns these days there are those who declare that they find God in nature. God is, for them, in the beauty of the sunrise and sunset, experienced in the clean smell of the air after a rain, embodied in the beauty of a flower. But what is one to say when nature turns upon us without cause? What is one to say about the devastation of tornadoes and floods? What about the droughts that erase the flowers from the landscape seemingly with no reason? What does the worshiper of nature say to that?

Whether in the proclamations of the prophet Isaiah or the words of the poets of the psalms or in the wisdom literature in which God accosts Job and speaks of his creative power, the scriptures keep God and nature apart except to discover in nature a witness to the one which brought it into being. The psalmist sums it up: "The heavens are telling the glory of God; and the firmament proclaims his handiwork" (Ps. 19:1).

> *"God becomes a caricature of ourselves, and we are victims of a deluded mind."*

To fashion an idol is an attempt to cut God down to size, to assume that God is susceptible to our control. All too many of us seek to reverse creation, and, rather than understanding ourselves to be in the image of God, make God over in our own image. For all too many of us, God is our color, our nationality, and favors our particular brand of religion. God becomes a caricature of ourselves, and we are victims of a deluded mind. Paul speaks of such persons in his letter to Rome:

> Though they knew God, they did not honor him as God or give thanks to him, but they became futile in their thinking, and their senseless minds were darkened. Claiming to be wise, they became fools; and they exchanged the glory of the immortal God for images resembling a mortal human being or birds or four-footed animals or reptiles. (Rom. 1:21-23)

Prophet and poet alike poke fun at such actions. The prophet Isaiah declares that all who make idols are nothing. His long description of the feverish activity of the person who cuts down a tree and carves a god from part of it and cooks his meal over the rest is hilarious—and meant to be: "No one considers, nor is there knowledge or discernment to say, 'Half of it I burned in the fire; I also baked bread on its coals, I roasted meat and have eaten. Now shall I make the rest of it an abomination? Shall I fall down before a block of wood?" (Isa. 44:19).

The psalmist contrasts the nature of the true God with fabricated images:

> Our God is in the heavens;
>   he does whatever he pleases.
> Their idols are silver and gold,
>   the work of human hands.
> They have mouths, but do not speak;
>   eyes, but do not see.
> They have ears, but do not hear;
>   noses, but do not smell.
> They have hands, but do not feel;
>   feet, but do not walk;
>   they make no sound in their throats.
> Those who make them are like them;
>   so are all who trust in them. (Ps. 115:3-8)

A keen insight regarding the matter of images is set out by Walter Harrelson in his book *The Ten Commandments and Human Rights*. Harrelson connects the matter of images with the reminder in Genesis that God has made us in his image, observing:

> Our temptation is not to identify the creature with the Creator, to claim a kind of power for our representation of God on earth that should not be claimed for any created thing. Our greater temptation is to miss the corollary of the second commandment; that God will have only one kind of representation on earth, one that is close to his very nature and power—human beings made in his image, and a community called out to embody this vocation before the nations of the earth (Walter Harrelson, *The Ten Commandments and Human Rights* [Philadelphia: Fortress Press,], p. 67).

Who can read Psalm 8 and not be caught up in the wonder of what God thinks of us? A little lower than God! Perhaps our greatest failure in connection with this command is that we do not live up to that image. Meant for the greater things in life, we abdicate our responsibility and turn to lesser things.

God thinks more of us than we think of ourselves!

> *"Each of us is privileged to represent God to the other."*

Given the opportunity to have dominion, we exploit and wound one another and the world in which we are privileged to live. Called to represent (by re-presenting) God to our neighbor in love, we turn a human face that seeks to use and to dominate. Offered the task of emissary and witness, we hide our credentials under the proverbial bushel and deny who we really are.

If the community that God intends is to be whole, if there is to be peace and concord, if there is to be unity, then that unity, that peace and concord, is given to those who take the matter of being in the image of God seriously. Each of us is privileged to represent God to the other. Each of us is called to be Christ to our neighbor. When that is so, we fulfill God's call to be in God's image, and the life of the community is bound together. When the people of God would make their pilgrimages to Jerusalem and run the risks and dangers present on the roads of that day, they would encourage themselves by repeating Psalm 121, which begins: "I lift up my eyes to the hills—from where will my help come?"

I think that a line may be left out. It was a line the pilgrim would have understood. Indulge me, and read it this way:

> I will lift my eyes to the hills—
> (where I see the pagan shrines
> from which the pagans gain strength),
> from where will my help come?

All around the people of Israel were those who placed their whitewashed shrines on hilltops so that they could look at them and take courage in time of danger. Allowed no such representations of Yahweh, the Israelite pilgrim would walk the same road and wonder: I can see where they get their courage. Where am I to find mine?

> *"Idolatry is our failure to present God's image in God's world."*

The next line differentiates between created gods and a God who creates: "My help comes from the LORD, who made heaven and earth" (Ps. 121:2). Contrary to what many think, it is not our fascination with cars and clothes and money and other outer symbols that hide the image of God in us that is idolatry.

Idolatry is our attempt to make God manageable, to cut God down to size. Idolatry is our failure to present God's image in God's world.

Read the commentary that comes with the command. I wonder whether Moses appended it, or whether some scribe in Babylon did it when the material was being fashioned into the Torah: "I the LORD your God am a jealous God, punishing children for the iniquity of parents, to the third and the fourth generation of those who reject me, but showing steadfast love to the thousandth generation of those who love me and keep my commandments" (Exod. 20:5*b*-6). It appears that the commentator was intent on exposing the grace of God as being much more pervasive than his wrath and judgment.

The author of the letter to the Ephesians makes an interesting comment when he addresses children: "Children, obey your parents in the Lord, for this is right. 'Honor your father and mother'—this is the first commandment with a promise" (Eph. 6:1-2).

Not so! In this second commandment we come face to face with a God whose love is everlasting, but whose wrath soon runs its course. God's mercy and love never end. Judgment soon runs its course; God's mercy and love never end.

This God wants to save us from small things and offers us a greater glory: God's own image in us, a reminder that we are created just a little lower than God, and a promise that those who catch that vision of themselves receive the fullest measure of love and can offer it to one another.

THE THIRD WORD

> *You shall not make wrongful use of the name of the LORD your God, for the LORD will not acquit anyone who misuses his name. (Exod. 20:7)*

What's in a Name?

I have a suspicion that what many of us imagine when we hear the third commandment is a little less than bizarre. The older translation of *wrongful use* as "vain" led many to associate the word with *vanity*, a word that once carried the connotation of profanity. The correct conclusion, then, was "Don't use God's name in connection with a curse word." Imagine, if you will, this rag-tag collection of recent slaves herded together at the foot of a smoking and quaking mountain to hear a word from the God who had brought them there, commanding, "Now it is okay to say damn, but don't say Yahweh damn." I do not mean to approve uncivilized profanity or defend loose talk, but when we hear only this message while listening to the third commandment, we succeed only in trivializing its meaning.

The name of God was sacred in Israel, so sacred that it went unspoken. To speak of the name was to express something of the being, or essence—to sum up the spirit and character of the named. One only has to recall that when persons were named among these people the names had to do with some special event surrounding their birth or some special plan or hope for the individual. Names were more than tags used to separate persons from one another, as names are used these days.

Alternative words were used for the name of God. We cannot even be sure about the pronunciation of the name of God as given in old manuscripts, because the word contained no vowels. YHWH (Y, H, W, H) became *Yahweh* when vowels were added in recent years to make it pronounceable. Yahweh was also expanded into the word *Jehovah,* which is still used by many in the Christian tradition.

> *"Names open doors and gain privileges."*

Names were considered powerful in Israel, and to use someone's name implied that some of the person's power (or prestige) came to the user. That ought not to surprise us. Many of us know all about asking someone to let us use his or her name as a reference, to mention his or her name when we think it will be helpful, to write a letter of recommendation and sign his or her name, to co-sign a promissory note and share responsibility with us. We know that names are powerful. Names open doors and gain privileges. Names perform deeds. To possess a name is to possess power, to be privy to the character and influence of that name.

The name of God is considered holy among the people of the scriptures. From the beginning of the Bible in history, the new population of the earth began to call upon the name of the Lord (Gen. 4:2-6). Prophets and poets praise, bless, and trust the name of the Lord (Pss. 69:30, 72:19; Isa. 50:10).

In the books of Genesis and Exodus, God is reported as taking three great risks. First, the risk of making human beings in God's image (Gen. 1:26), then giving them dominion (Gen. 1:26). Above all else, perhaps, he revealed his name (Exod. 3:13-15). Our lives, the world, and God's reputation are placed in our hands. Those of us who claim to be children of God bring honor or dishonor on the name of

God (character, being, essence, person, image) by what we do with these gifts.

Perhaps the way we most wrongfully use God's name is our taking the name and yet not living a life that honors that name. How many wear a golden cross around the neck or on the lapel, but never consider emulating the sacrifice to which it witnesses?

When considering this matter, one cannot help thinking of those who solemnly gather at the altar of the church and take vows of membership, promising to support the church and its mission with prayers, presence, time, and treasure, and then are seldom seen or heard of afterward. Or consider those who bring their infant children to the sanctuary and there make solemn promises to rear the children in a home and church atmosphere that will lead them to lives of faithfulness, and then promptly go home and forget the vows, treating the occasion as if it were some family holiday or social obligation. How many times have we watched as two young persons, faces flushed with love and devotion, stand amid the beauty of the wedding ceremony and make promises in the name of the Father, Son, and Holy Spirit, and then live as if God had nothing to do with their lives?

We in the church are challenged to make such vows meaningful again. We point out to those who take vows that there is the great risk that dishonor may be brought on the name of God. Can it be that renewal in the life of the church can come only when we make the vows people take mean something, and warn them that if they do not mean to keep these vows they take them at their spiritual peril? We cannot expect others to take the vows seriously if the church does not.

> *"Praise and practice are inseparable for the faithful."*

Jesus must have had this commandment in mind when he declared: "Not everyone who says to me, 'Lord, Lord,' will enter the kingdom of heaven, but only the one who does the will of my Father in heaven" (Matt. 7:21).

Praise and practice are inseparable for the faithful. The old cliché, "What you do speaks so loudly that I cannot hear what you have to say," may be spoken to some of us by God, who knows that these two do not match in our lives.

It is one thing to stand in the pew on Sunday and sing "Holy, Holy, Holy"; it is quite another to practice holiness in our daily conduct. While it may be assumed that this command can, in the strictest sense, refer to formal oath taking, it surely must be linked with things that are just as important and that take place each day of our lives. One immediately thinks of such oaths as "by God" or "in the name of God." But what about those moments when we are frustrated by what life brings to us, when we are disappointed by the failure to gain some coveted thing, those times when some unexpected destructive thing happens and we involve God both in our thoughts and in our words? You hear it every day: "I prayed about that for months, and God did not answer my prayer"; "God promised the life abundant, and I have had nothing but hard times"; "Somebody must have done some evil thing to provoke God to do that to those people"; "I just knew that if they continued to live that way, something bad was going to happen."

Sometimes we make wrongful use of the name of God by attributing things to God that are contrary to what is made known to us in Jesus Christ. Often, even in the church, we hear the assumption made that God "has it in" for the sinner and showers blessings on those who are good.

One has only to measure such a conclusion against the words of Jesus:

> You have heard that it was said, "You shall love your neighbor and hate your enemy." But I say to you, Love your enemies and pray for those who persecute you, so that you may be children

of your Father in heaven; for he makes his sun rise on the evil and on the good, and sends rain on the righteous and on the unrighteous. (Matt. 5:43-45)

Everyone is treated the same by God. It makes good sense to me that if sun and rain are given without favor, then the sunstroke and the rainstorm are likewise given. God does not play favorites, and neither should we. Jesus concludes with the words: "Be perfect, therefore, as your heavenly Father is perfect" (Matt. 5:48).

How tragic it is that all too many commentators on this line reduce its meaning to some small dimension of moralism and suggest that we are under some compulsion to be as morally perfect as God. Even God knows better than that, as the poet reveals: "He knows how we were made; he remembers that we are dust" (Ps. 103:14). God remembers; we forget.

> *"To display altruistic perfection is to give honor to the name of God."*

To be perfect as God is perfect is to love as God loves, without favor and without holding back. To display altruistic perfection is to give honor to the name of God.

Few biblical writers take the matter of God's name as seriously as does the writer of the book of Revelation. As chapter 22 opens, the vision of the River of Life, which flows through the New Jerusalem, is described, and then the writer says of the servants of God: "They will see his face, and his name will be on their foreheads" (Rev. 22:4). Here the writer of Revelation joins with the writer of Hebrews in describing what God thinks and will do for the faithful.

Chapter 11 of the book of Hebrews is a witness to a long line of those who were faithful in every sort of circumstance in life. The chapter opens naming Abel, Enoch, Noah, Abraham, and Sarah and then pauses midlist to summarize: "All of these died in faith without having received the promises, but from a distance they saw and greeted them. They confessed that they were strangers and foreigners on the earth. . . . *Therefore God is not ashamed to be called their God*" (Heb. 11:13, 16*b*, italics added). Can you imagine a greater accolade?

These are the people who have brought honor on the name of God; they have been steadfast in their witness and in their living; they have done nothing to cause others to doubt God's faithfulness and grace. Here we discover the other side of the commandment. Those who are careless about God's reputation are not acquitted (are guilty), while those who do take great care for what their lives reflect of God's character discover that God is proud to be their God. Perhaps Jesus had this command in mind when he said: "Let your light shine before others, so that they may see your good works and give glory to your Father in heaven" (Matt. 5:16).

When I was a boy, there were, as is the case for most of us, times when my conduct did not measure up to my father's expectations. He maintained that I was learning bad habits from my associates. When he could tolerate no more, he would sit me down and say, "Tell me your name." I knew what was coming and would protest, but he would persist, "Tell me your name." I would reply, "Ross." "No," he would say, I mean your last name. Again I would respond, "Marrs." "Spell it," he would say, and then I would spell it slowly, "M—A—R—R—S." "Now," he would say, "does that sound like Wilson or James or Altizer?" "No," I would confess. Then he would drive the lesson home: "Then you are not a Wilson or a James or an Altizer, and you are expected not to act like one."

The lesson still stands. It stands for each of us.

What is your name?

And we answer, "Christian."

Spell it!

C—H—R—I—S—T—I—A—N!

Then live like a Christian. Never wrongfully use Christ's name.

THE FOURTH WORD

*Remember the sabbath day, and keep it holy.
Six days you shall labor and do all your work.
But the seventh day is a sabbath to the LORD
your God; you shall not do any work—you,
your son or your daughter, your male or female
slave, your livestock, or the alien resident in your
towns. For in six days the LORD made heaven
and earth, the sea, and all that is in them, but
rested the seventh day; therefore the LORD
blessed the sabbath day and consecrated it.
(Exod. 20:8-11)*

A Link Between Heaven and Earth

The word *sabbath* means "to cease, to stop, to rest." I grew up in a community and in a home where Christians were supposed to take the fourth commandment seriously. It did not matter that Saturday was really the sabbath referred to in the command; the meaning of sabbath had been long since given to Sunday for us. Sunday was supposed to be kept holy, and the word *holy* means "different." Sunday was meant to be different from the other six days of the week. No work, only quiet play and not too much fun on Sunday. Sunday was always a mixed blessing for me. Perhaps because the children of Israel received two day's supply of manna on Friday to tide them over the sabbath, my father required me to do two days of chores on Saturday in order to avoid working on Sunday.

There was a man in our community who considered the fourth command foolishness. Every Sunday he and his boys went to the fields to plant or to hoe corn and potatoes just as they would on any other day. I remember the older people in our town saying, "You'll see, he'll get no crop. It won't make. You'll see!" A lot of explaining was in order in the fall when Mr. Christian (I swear that was his name) and his boys carried great sacks of corn and potatoes off that hill—on Sundays!

> *"My father required me to do two days of chores in order to avoid working on Sunday."*

Probably no other commandment has had such a controversial history. The observance of the day may have had its beginnings in some primitive superstition about the seventh day being unlucky because the gods frowned on anyone doing much on their day. Where it had its beginning does not matter so much as what the Hebrews did with it. In their usual sensible style, with God's help, they turned a negative into a positive, turned a day of fear and superstition into a day of joy and celebration, a day meant to mark God's great acts of grace on behalf of his people. Both in the Exodus account, which links that grace with God's creation of all existence, including Israel, and in the account in Deuteronomy 5, which links that grace with their deliverance from bondage in Egypt, the focus is on God's mighty acts. But soon, of course, the moralists and the legalists took hold of it. What began as a privilege became an obligation and a rule, an institution. Instead of being a sign of what God had done for them, keeping the sabbath became a way they showed what they were willing to do for God. Those who laid hold of the day and robbed it of its best meanings spun out their endless detail on how to properly observe the sabbath. William Barclay comments:

> The Sabbath Law was very complicated and very detailed. The commandment forbids work on the Sabbath day; but the interpreters of the Law were not satisfied with that simple prohibition. Work had to be defined. So thirty-nine basic actions were laid down, which were forbidden on the sabbath, and amongst them were reaping, winnowing and threshing, and preparing a meal. (William Barclay, *The Daily Bible Study Guide: Matthew,* rev. ed. [Philadelphia: Westminster, 1975], p. 22)

When discussing the Maccabean revolt 170 years before Christ, Barclay reports:

> In the time of the uprising under Judas Maccabaeus, certain Jews sought refuge in the caves in the wilderness. Antiochus sent a detachment of men to attack them; the attack was made on the Sabbath day; and these insurgent Jews died without even a gesture of defiance or defence, because to fight would have been to break the Sabbath. (Barclay, *The Daily Bible Study Guide,* p. 28)

> ## *"When it came to the sabbath, the legalists stayed on the job."*

By the time of Jesus, keeping the sabbath had become so entangled with constrictions and details that keeping the day was a hopeless matter for most. Only full-time religious people could hope to come near to complete observance of the day. For example, in the Gospels we discover that Jesus was continually embroiled in controversy with the legalists over the keeping of the sabbath. The fact that these reports persist in all of the Gospels indicates that controversy over the sabbath was not only a sore point between Jesus and the Pharisees, but also continued to be a main point of contention between the early Christian community and the synagogue for most of the first century. It is clear that the early church took issue with the legalists in both church and synagogue. In fact, by the end of the first century the early church turned away from observance of the sabbath, dropped all the legalisms, and shifted their day of rest and worship to the first day of the week, Sunday, and began to focus attention on God's mighty act in the resurrection. But, of course, you can bet on the legalists and the moralists. Anxious to please God by their demonstrated righteousness, when it came to the sabbath the legalists stayed on the job.

In 321 CE the Emperor Constantine declared Sunday to be a day of rest. Work was to cease in the countryside, while it could continue in the cities. Christian soldiers were to worship; non-Christian soldiers had to march in parade. By the eighth century the work of the legalists bore fruit when a church leader declared that the sabbath and Sunday were identical in their meaning and requirement. The legalisms continued until the reformers tried to free the day from its shackles. John Calvin spoke for reform: "The Sabbath is abrogated. It being expedient to overthrow superstition, the Jewish holy day was abolished, and as a thing necessary to retain decency, order and peace in the church, another day was appointed for that purpose. The observance of days among us is a free service and free of all superstition." (See William Barclay, *The Ten Commandments for Today* [New York: Harper & Row, 1983], pp. 34-35.) But the sabbatarians won the day. The Puritans of England identified Sunday as the Sabbath and passed rules to enforce it. In the Westminster Confession of 1648, they declared:

> This Sabbath is then kept holy unto the Lord, when men, after due preparing of their hearts, and ordering of their common affairs beforehand, do not only observe an holy rest all the day from their own works, words and thoughts about their worldly employment and recreations; but also are taken up the whole

time in the public and private exercises of his worship, and in the duties of necessity and mercy. (Barclay, *The Ten Commandments for Today*, pp. 36-37)

That declaration is not far removed from the small-town and rural backgrounds of many in the church today.

But then the world changed. The industrial revolution, the rise of great cities, international travel, modern warfare, new ways and standards of living and expectation—all these changes and greater technology brought pressure against those who insisted on keeping Sunday free from any work, until it seems that the entire idea has been abandoned as out-of-date, unworkable, impossible, and irrelevant. Now it seems that no one is greatly concerned about the fourth commandment.

T. S. Eliot draws a word picture of the church in industrialized England that is not far removed from the situation in our own country. In "Choruses from 'The Rock,'" he writes,

I journeyed to London, to the timekept City,
Where the River flows, with foreign flotations.
There I was told: we have too many churches,
And too few chop-houses. There I was told:
Let the vicars retire. Men do not need the Church
In the place where they work, but where they spend their
    Sundays.
In the City we need no bells:
Let them waken the suburbs.
I journeyed to the suburbs, and there I was told:
We toil for six days, and on the seventh we must motor
To Hindhead, or Maidenhead.
If the weather is foul we stay at home and read the papers.
In industrial districts, there I was told
Of economic laws.
In the pleasant countryside, there it seemed
That the country now is only fit for picnics.
And the Church does not seem to be wanted
In country or in suburbs; and in the town
Only for important weddings.

45

But have we gone too far? Have we so reacted to legalistic and distorted interpretations of this command that we ignore it altogether, and in the process miss the message that was heard long ago, the message that ought to be heard today?

As was mentioned in the introduction of this book, these commandments were for a new community in two ways. First, they were not commandments to which obedience was required so that God would accept these people. Rather, the instructions were given as a way of responding to a God who had already taken initiative and done great things for them. God had called their ancestors Abraham and Sarah to a new land. God had been with Isaac and Rachel and Jacob and Rebecca. And God had brought their ancestors out of bondage with a mighty hand.

The One who had created all things, the Lord of the universe, had come to them, a rag-tag, anxious, and weary band of slaves standing half-naked at the foot of Mount Sinai, and made a covenant with them. God chose them to be the instrument of God's grace, offered to all nations. God's commandments were reminders first of all of what God had done for them and how their lives were to be lived as their response to his grace.

Second, these words were not a list of commands given to individuals so that they could please God. Rather, the words were a part of God's design for making a community, for bringing the nation into existence and thus creating the people of God.

These commands must be honored if the people of God are to become a new community, whether after the exodus or after the exile or after the modern industrial revolution.

We have already seen how the first three commandments declare that any true community is anchored in loyalty, obedience, and allegiance to God.

> You shall have no other Gods before me.
> You shall not make for yourself an idol.
> You shall not make wrongful use of the name of the Lord
>   your God.

46

That theme continues in the fourth commandment: Remember the sabbath day, and keep it holy.

How do we keep it holy? In Genesis 2 we read the conclusion of the first creation story:

> Thus the heavens and the earth were finished, and all their multitude. And on the seventh day God finished the work that he had done, and he rested on the seventh day from all the work that he had done. So God blessed the seventh day and hallowed it, because on it God rested from all the work that he had done in creation. (Gen. 2:1-3)

The sabbath is a day for remembering God's great works, for focusing attention on undeserved works of grace, deliverance, and salvation. Paul helped the Romans to understand this matter: "Some judge one day to be better than another, while others judge all days to be alike. Let all be fully convinced in their own minds. Those who observe the day, observe it in honor of the Lord" (Rom. 14:5-6*a*).

> *"The fourth commandment is a bridge or a link between God and the human race, between heaven and earth, between work and worship."*

The purpose of the command is centered in the well-being of persons. Jesus said it succinctly: "The sabbath was made for humankind, and not humankind for the sabbath; so the Son of Man is Lord even of the sabbath" (Mark 2:27-28). In an unavoidable way, the fourth commandment is a bridge or a link between God and the human race, between heaven and earth, between work and worship. This is a commandment focused in the well-being of the whole community because it takes the individual seriously.

Some imagine that it is our place to demean and devalue ourselves in the presence of a holy and majestic God. We are

47

to consider ourselves as worms in the dust and all our works as worthless in God's economy. In Psalm 8, the poet of Israel takes a contrary position and tells us what God thinks of us: "You have made them a little lower than God, and crowned them with glory and honor" (Ps. 8:5).

Community begins with loyalty and obedience to God. Community finds strength for cohesiveness when there is a proper concern for men and women and all of their needs— needs for body, mind, and spirit.

Like religious people of all ages, we seem to like to put our emphasis on things of the spirit and talk of spiritual things. Neither the Hebrew scriptures nor the New Testament separates the spirit out from life in such a manner. Biblical concern is concern for the whole person. Rest! Take care of yourself, your whole person.

Paul echoes the command in his letter to Rome: "I appeal to you therefore, brothers and sisters, by the mercies of God, to present your bodies as a living sacrifice, holy and acceptable to God, which is your spiritual worship" (Rom. 12:1). Jesus echoed this concern for persons as being greater than concern for legalism when he asked his detractors: "I ask you, is it lawful to do good or to do harm on the sabbath, to save life or to destroy it?" (Luke 6:9). If there is to be community, if we are to be the people of God, then there must be a concern for the wholeness of each individual.

> *"Our present-day fascination with the body, to the neglect of the mind, is akin to a new idolatry."*

Look at us! Most of us grow and mature physically because we have little choice. Some of us act as if we are all meat and bone and give great attention to the body. Our present-day fascination with the body, to the neglect of the mind, is akin to a new idolatry. Too many of us read our last book or did our last thinking at about age eighteen or twenty. And we quit church and that churchy stuff at fourteen or fifteen. And here we are: fifty in body, twenty or so in mind, and fourteen in spirit. Little wonder we come apart at the seams so readily. We are not whole. Little wonder the community is fragmented when it is composed of people who are fragmented.

We talk of our need for recreation. So we charge out on a weekend and spend ourselves in what would better be called wreckreation, which is not what I mean by fascination with the body. Take another look at the word *recreation*. It means re-creation, doing those things that restore and build up and make strong the whole person. (By the way, that might mean that we should work on the sabbath. All too many of us are sedentary all week, and perhaps we ought to observe this command by finding a way to sweat on Sunday.)

This is a commandment just for you and me. It was given, not so we can grow more spiritual and prove our acceptability to God, but so we can become the whole persons God intends us to be. The fourth command was given so that we can be part of the community into which God calls us, that community in which we are nurtured as children of love and mercy and are called to share the grace given us with others.

As Christians, we have something special to offer in connection with this command. For us, God's mightiest act of all was the resurrection of our Lord. Maybe we ought to bring the command up to date and rewrite it. It is all right to rewrite it and bring it up to date. In Exodus the rationale is attached to creation. In Deuteronomy (5:12-15) the writer comes down heavily on the side of the well-being of persons. The prophet Ezekiel adds a dimension: "I the LORD am your God; follow my statutes, and be careful to observe my ordinances, and hallow my sabbaths so that they may be a sign between me and you, so that you may know that I the LORD am your God" (Ezek. 20:19-20). For Ezekiel, the day is a sign of the covenant.

In every case the scriptures are deliberate in linking the day with God's mighty acts on behalf of his people—creation, deliverance, and covenant.

How fortunate we are to hear that. How fortunate for us for whom God's greatest act is the resurrection. We are in church and at worship on Sunday because for us Sunday is meant to be holy, different, because of the resurrection. Perhaps we ought to rewrite the commandment something like this:

Remember Sunday as a day to be observed differently from other days. On that day you shall remember that God raised Jesus from the dead, defeated the powers of death, and made us all heirs of life eternal. All of this is for your sake. Therefore, since God loves you so much, love yourself, take care of yourself, and do those things that make for wholeness of body, mind, and spirit.

This is your day.

THE FIFTH WORD

Honor your father and your mother, so that your days may be long in the land that the LORD your God is giving you.
(Exod. 20:12)

Focus on the Family

A fearful, dissatisfied, murmuring, tired band of recently freed slaves, heirs to more than four centuries of bondage in Egypt have been swept off their feet by wonderful promises made by a man whom they hardly know and whose connection with the palace makes him highly suspect. They know the story about his killing the Egyptian, and some must be wondering whether that was a put-up job to deceive them into thinking he was anti-Egyptian. They have been dazzled by all the plagues visited on the Egyptians—that would impress most people. Then, before they can make plans or get ready, they are suddenly uprooted from their daily routine and the security of a roof and meals and led out into a wilderness where hunger and thirst and fear dog their every step. Finally they are brought to a mountain, which this Moses seems to think is sacred, and there they are commanded to stand ready and obedient while he climbs up the mountain to talk to his exclusive and invisible God.

One can understand the rationale for the first three commandments. These commandments to have no other gods, to make no images, and not to use God's name in an unworthy manner make sense if this really is the only true God, who has dominance over all other gods.

51

The fourth commandment to observe the sabbath is good news to these slaves who have had to work seven days a week in Egypt. You can almost hear them whisper to one another, "Now there is a good one. I like that one. We can use a day off."

Then, it appears, according to the imagining of many, that Moses, in the middle of reading these words from God, says something like, "Now, you older folks move back there a bit and let the children come up front. It's time for the children's sermon. Now, children, come on up front. Yes, that's right, just sit down there on the grass. I have a special word from God that is just for you, 'Honor your father and your mother, so that your days may be long in the land that the LORD your God is giving to you.' "

That sounds amusing and a bit silly, doesn't it? And it is. Yet, that is the way we often interpret the command to honor our parents, as if it were a sermon just for little children. Even the writer of the Ephesian letter used it in this manner when he wrote: " 'Children, obey your parents in the Lord, for this is right. Honor your father and mother'—this is the first commandment with a promise" (Eph. 6:1-2).

Who can argue with the simple reminder that parents ought to be honored by their children? When we observe the scene in many homes these days, we are increasingly tempted to focus the attention in this direction and make the most of it. We could do with more obedience to this command among children, and we could stand to match it with a greater effort on the part of the parents to be worthy of the honor. But to pursue this limited meaning is to step into a quagmire of "ifs" and "buts" and "howevers" as we begin to argue about parents who do not merit honor and children who are given less than they ought to receive.

Remember, this is a people being led toward a new land and a new experience—whether it is the recently freed slaves of Egypt or whether it is those returning to their homeland after the exile to Babylon. For our purposes here, we will stick with the story as it is presented in Exodus.

It was to be a long time coming, but it is clear that it is God's intent to make these fragmented people into one people. Community is something with which they have had little experience. They will be charting a course into the unexplored, and the commandments and other laws are meant to provide guidelines for the day when they will live in towns and cities and their life-styles will be greatly different. One thing that is going to be changed is the shape of the family. When they were slaves, family was not a vital reality to them. Each person was owned by the Egyptians. They could be killed or set free at the will of the owner. In addition, their security and their daily lives did not depend on the economic clout of a family. Their food, clothing, shelter, jobs—everything—was provided, limited, and dictated by the Egyptians.

Now they were headed into a new land, called to take new responsibility for themselves and for one another. Now the family would become a key element in the stability of the community. Things would be greatly changed. They would be responsible for one another; they would depend on one another; and there would be a special new problem that had not been theirs before.

No doubt little children would continue to be of concern and would be cared for. Active and contributing members of the family would be able to deal with one another and to look out for one another. But the one group that was going to be especially at risk in the new land would be the elderly. There would be no overseers to watch out for them, no easy jobs, such as those available in Egypt. The elderly would be placed at risk in the new land.

The fifth commandment took on special significance for those elderly persons and their children who stood at Sinai. In the new land the strong and the able would be caught up in a myriad of tasks associated with pushing out the current ruling classes of the land, getting settled, and organizing a new community. It was likely that the old folks would fall through the cracks, be put on the shelf, declared excess, imposing great burdens, and would be left to fend for themselves as best they could. Sound familiar? Sound contemporary?

> "This command was not given to little children. It was meant for grown people."

Now, hear the command: "Honor your father and your mother." This command was not given to little children. It was meant for grown people, for mature men and women who would face the new problem of providing for aging parents in their new cities and towns.

What command could be more contemporary? What command could speak to our current moment in history with more relevance? In a real sense we are like those slaves standing at the bottom of Sinai and at the edge of a new experience.

We do not need to be burdened with statistics about the growth of longevity and the increase in the number of elderly in our present day. All of us are aware of the heated discussions that go on in our midst about housing, adequate health care, and extended services that are required for this special group of persons. Every day the media serve up a menu of horror stories about evictions, death by exposure, mistreatment by families and in nursing homes, inadequate facilities, and escalating costs. We are made terribly uncomfortable when we are involved in discussions of euthanasia, whether passive or active. In a knee-jerk reaction, we have passed laws that inflict needless suffering on deteriorating elderly persons in the name of preserving life. We are engaged in hot debate about costs, about whether certain procedures ought to be made available, and all of us have added new words to our vocabulary, such as *senility* and *Alzheimer's disease*. We are keenly aware of the personal burdens imposed by arthritis, neuralgias, loss of energy, and loneliness. And we are repeatedly reminded that the stage is being set for conflict between the elderly segment of our society and the younger as more and more grow older and require more and more care, fewer will be available to bear the cost.

The fifth commandment is forever a contemporary word: *Honor your father and your mother.* Any people who mean to be a community that lasts must be a people who care for the elderly. We need to consider the whole command: "Honor your father and your mother, so that your days may be long in the land that the LORD your God is giving you."

Too often we have heard this command interpreted to mean that if children are obedient they will live a long time as a reward. *Nonsense!* This command is not addressed to individuals. Rather, it and the others are addressed to a people. Any people, any society, any nation that does not care for the aging in its midst is a people or a society or a nation destined for a short life span.

Jesus faced this problem. There were those in his day who sought to avoid responsibilities. Some would take advantage of a rule that said that whatever had been dedicated to God could not be claimed by anyone else. Addressing the Pharisees and some of the scribes who had come from Jerusalem to harass him, Jesus said:

> You have a fine way of rejecting the commandment of God in order to keep your tradition! For Moses said, "Honor your father and your mother"; and, "Whoever speaks evil of father or mother must surely die." But you say that if anyone tells father or mother, "Whatever support you might have had from me is Corban" (that is, an offering to God)—then you no longer permit doing anything for a father or mother, thus making void the word of God through your tradition that you have handed on. (Mark 7:9-13)

Clearly no one is certain of what the solutions to current problems related to aging must be. Clearly these matters will require our careful attention in the years to come, and we will probably surprise ourselves as the solutions emerge. We

55

must continue to discuss and debate, to experiment and work together in order to be faithful to the needs of those who inevitably grow older, leave the work force, live alone, are bereft of the support of the extended family, and have no place to turn when health fails. Any society that abandons its aging population will soon fall on evil days, and the society that takes its aging persons seriously is promised and will gain long life.

This command, in a very real way says something to us by what it takes for granted and does not say. It is clear that the commandment assumes that children will be taken care of and that husbands and wives will care for each other. It is not said, but it is clearly implied. Thus the commandment not only addresses the specific problem of the aging, but it also relates to the entire family. The fifth commandment maintains that the family is an essential ingredient in the binding of a people into a community.

Gradually the design of the commands is coming clear. The first three commandments declare that single-hearted devotion and allegiance to one God are required as a base for community. A people cannot find unity running off in every direction, following after every god. The fourth commandment expresses concern for the individual in the community. Those societies that seek wholeness and longevity must be societies that take into consideration the wholeness of every individual. The command to observe the sabbath focuses our attention on the individual. The message is clear: Community is built on (1) the worship of one God, (2) concern for the individual, and (3) concern for the family.

> *"You cannot have one person without three."*

When we listen to the cacophony of voices ringing the bells of doom for the family these days, we hear the alarm being sounded. Divorce, working parents, models proposed by the media, new marital arrangements that seem foreign to good sense, the loss of the extended family, outside influences that invade what was once private—these and other causes are named as the culprits that assault the family. A myriad of solutions is proposed, and discussions rage on every hand, but central to everything, underlying every attempted solution, critical to every recommendation, must be the understanding that the family is a key element in the establishing of community. It is clear that God intended the family. You cannot have one person without three. No scientific invention for the test tube is likely to get around that requirement. Moreover, the extended period of dependence on the part of new arrivals argues for the family as an order of creation. Whatever form it takes, however we shape and reshape it, the family is basic to humanness and to community.

Most of us would no doubt agree that humanness does not come from just being born. The family, the home, is entrusted with the task nurturing, shaping, and molding the whole person who is to become a part of the larger community. The home is the crucible in which character is formed in the heat of close confrontation and in the warmth of caring love.

Another metaphor comes to mind. It is no exaggeration to say that the home is the spiritual placenta from which individuals gain the nourishment that brings them to maturity. Any community, any society, any nation that imagines that the task and the role of the home can successfully be assigned to mercenaries and substitutes is a society, nation, and community that cannot hope for the promise that comes with the command.

Honor your father and your mother. Take care of the aging. And take care of the young and one another. When the home and the community join forces and support that which makes for full humanness, then the promise of long and meaningful life will be God's gift for those who have made the commitment.

THE SIXTH WORD

You shall not murder. (Exod. 20:13)

What God Thinks of Us

The New Revised Standard Version of the Bible narrows this command a bit from its older form in the RSV, "You shall not kill." In its older form, it seemed to be a prohibition against any kind of killing, whether accidental or intentional. The new form places its emphasis on intent, the spirit behind the act. This narrowing of the command offers those of us who live in a complicated world some breathing space as we seek to face up to issues that are specifically ours.

Even so, we must begin with what the command implies when it is first spoken by Moses at Mount Sinai. One wonders how this man could bring such a word after he had killed an Egyptian overseer who was beating one of his kinsfolk. Furthermore, how could he bring this word to a people who knew about his background? (See Exod. 2:11ff.) Life must have been cheap among the labor gangs of Egypt. For a long time these people had enjoyed a peaceful and prosperous time as long as the invading Hyksos ruled in Egypt. But then, according to Exodus 1:8, "A new king arose over Egypt, who did not know Joseph." The Egyptians recovered control of their nation in 1580 BCE and under Rameses II had undertaken a great national building program.

Like other nations in that part of the world, Egypt was not hesitant to put other peoples in slavery in order to accomplish its projects. The people of Joseph had lost their friend in courts, and in Exodus we learn of their harsh bondage and cry to God, which set in motion their deliverance.

Now things are different. At Sinai they face new realities and new possibilities. God knows, even if they do not, that they are headed for difficult days. There will be hardships to endure, battles to be won, and new hopes and aspirations will arise in their midst. Moreover they will be going into lands where life is cheap and where human sacrifice is practiced. It is critical that they understand that things are meant to be different for them in the new land. This God of Sinai holds life sacred. For this God, persons are not expendable but are to be treated as valuable. We have already discovered something of what this God thinks of us, who made us in his image, who has given us dominion, and has entrusted us with his name.

> *"One wonders how this man could bring such a word after he had killed an Egyptian overseer."*

In one of the earliest stories in Genesis we read of God's coming to Cain and asking him about the welfare of his brother, Abel, whom Cain has killed. God does not take this matter lightly and places a curse on Cain. In one line God's wrath burns hot, but in the next his act of grace reveals divine regard for life: "The LORD put a mark on Cain, so that no one who came upon him would kill him" (Gen. 4:15).

I remember once hearing it said that the mark of Cain was the mark of a murderer. Not here. This is God's mark, a mark meant to protect Cain. Here we discover God's grace overcoming wrath and telling us something about what God thinks of us.

I know of no better word about what God thinks of us than that in Psalm 8, which begins with a declaration of the majesty and glory of God. Over against that majesty, you might expect that human beings would be portrayed as not amounting to very much. Just the opposite is true. The psalmist sees that majesty and exclaims:

> When I look at your heavens,
>   the work of your fingers,
> the moon and the stars that
>   you have established;
> what are human beings that you
>   are mindful of them,
>   mortals that you care for them?
> Yet, you have made them a little
>   lower than God,
> and crowned them with glory
>   and honor.
> You have given them dominion
> over the works of your hands. (Ps. 8:3-6*a*)

Of course, there are many stories in the Old Testament that seem to contradict this notion of the sacredness of life. A great flood clears the world of the wicked; Israel is commanded to lay waste to evil nations; death is decreed for certain violations of the law. We can only leave these stories to relate to their own age and not judge them by our Christian standards.

In short, the sixth commandment maintains that life is a gift of God's hand. Life, therefore, is sacred to God and is not to be taken lightly. This is a sobering word to a world such as ours. Everyday we are confronted with new stories of violence done to life that shock our sensibilities and demand that we do something to make things different.

We have long been engaged in a national debate about whether capital punishment is acceptable in a civilized world, and whether we ought to entrust the state with such power. The long-standing uproar over abortion has led some to think that we are polarized over this issue, when the truth is that most of the noise we hear is either from a minority on one extreme or the other—with both extremes seeking certainty and security from a hard and fast position. The majority of us are not quite so sure, and we favor a middle position that says both yes and no, depending on the circumstances.

Debates over whether wars are justifiable have been raging for decades. We are still seeking to bind up the nation's wounds, which have resulted from our disagreements on this matter.

Euthanasia, either passive or active, has become all too familiar to us, and we are alarmed at the possibilities that lie before us. Suicide is now being discussed as an alternative to the assaults that AIDS and Alzheimer's disease unleash on many.

We are a people groping for answers, hoping for simple solutions that are not likely to come. Persons holding opposite positions base their arguments on a search for human dignity. It may be that the nation will arrive at legal solutions that suit none, and offer options that are repugnant to many. It may well be that what the variegated body politic of this nation can accept and what the courts may declare constitutional will not square with our Judeo-Christian understanding of the origin and destiny of the human race. As Christians, we may find ourselves living in a nation that does not share our convictions; we may be called upon to offer our witness by pursuing options that for us are moral, while they may be illegal, and avoiding options that for us are immoral, while they may be legal.

One of the problems we encounter everyday, and that in some measure illustrates an essential problem of a democracy, is that we seem bent on morality by majority vote, whether in legislatures or in courts of law. The media bombard us with studies and surveys that support one position or another. It seems that many conclude that a thing is right if "everybody does it."

> ## "We have sought to deal with our problems by identifying degrees of murder."

New possibilities are made available by our expanding scientific knowledge and with our increasing interdependent situation as residents on this space ship we call earth. War, which once was limited to the combatants, then spread to general populations, now takes on sinister dimensions as those beyond the boundaries of the combatants may be victimized. Radiation and gas poisoning join with bacterial onslaughts that cannot be restricted to lines on a map and increase our potential for killing. Even the continued use of fossil fuels for transportation and to drive the wheels of industry may someday be more clearly identified as components of both murder and suicide. We have sought to deal with our problems by identifying degrees of murder and applying every technology available in our efforts to decide between what is justifiable and what is not.

People must have been wrestling with the same gordian knots when Jesus was on earth. One can bet that the scribes had spun out a multitude of wherefores and whereases regarding this matter. Jesus, in his usual simple and uncomplicated style, challenged all the hair splitting and swept away all the discussions in his commentary on killing in the Sermon on the Mount.

> You have heard that it was said to those of ancient times, "You shall not murder"; and "whoever murders shall be liable to judgment." But I say to you that if you are angry with a brother or sister, you will be liable to judgment; and if you insult a brother or sister, you will be liable to the council; and if you say, "You fool," you will be liable to the hell of fire. (Matt. 5:21-22)

Jesus' words were startling then, and they would surely still be startling to many if we demanded that they be followed literally.

We worry about being brought before the law courts and there being accused of murder. Jesus, however, reminds us that we stand before an entirely different court, a court in which the judge knows our hearts. For Jesus it is more important to pursue the spirit of the law rather than the letter of the law.

This makes the matter much clearer for each of us and gives us firmer ground for our decisions. Although we are not perfect judges of our intentions, and most often are masters of self-deception, those of us who are seeking God's will know that we can come into God's presence and sort things out within our Christian community. Of course, that does not justify every conclusion we reach. There are persons to be considered other than ourselves. This command not to commit murder has particular meaning for a community. It serves to remind us of the positive side of the command, which calls for us to take life seriously, to treat it as sacred, to regard each person as a recipient of life from the hand of God and as one who is entitled to protection of that life.

If Israel was to establish the covenant community intended by God, that meant that the people had to hold life sacred and take every step to preserve and enhance it. They had to establish an environment in which everyone was safe and protected.

But the command meant more than that. It also meant that every person had a right to a quality of life that gave life meaning. Being alive is not the definition of life. Life in community requires more: freedom, justice, love, acceptance, meaning.

These same guidelines must be at the heart of any decision we make in our own day. We must hold life sacred because it is so regarded by God. We must deal with our attitudes toward one another at the point of origin, at the point of our intent and spirit. We must learn that merely to preserve life is not fulfilling the best intent of the command. Rather, we support the need and the means for making life promising and abundant.

Our potential for killing one another and rationalizing it are greater than ever before. None of us is exempt. Our very solidarity with one another makes us party to much we would not support. As taxpayers, we cannot pick and choose what we will support, and so we are caught up in the acts of the nation. As voters, we cannot know all about the candidates we support, and yet we make their actions, both the good and the bad, possible.

In this imperfect world, we are under command to do all we can to discover God's will for ourselves—and follow it. Our imperfect knowledge and understanding, joined with that of others, makes us fallible. Because of that fallibility, we are indeed persons "standing in the need of prayer," persons whose only hope is grace.

Jesus knows us well and understands our potential for rationalization and self-delusion. We are not allowed to spend much time testing the winds of opinion or weaving a myriad of laws for clarification. Jesus leads us into the presence of God and there opens our hearts for examination.

It is in the presence of the God he has made known to us that we can face our questions unafraid. And it is to that God that we can bring our fallibility and imperfections and still know that we are made worthy to come into his presence, simply because he would have it so.

THE SEVENTH WORD

You shall not commit adultery. (Exod. 20:14)

The Need for a People Who Blush

I f we were to restrict this commandment to its original meaning it would say, "No married woman is to have sexual relationships with any man other than her husband." There is little doubt that while we have expanded this commandment to embrace almost every form of sexual behavior, in its original form it had to do with the stability of the community and ensuring the home as a place for the nurturing of children. The very existence of this command is at the heart of what is necessary for the survival of any community, and no community can endure when there is disdain and disregard for the sanctity of the relationship that lies most closely to procreation and the nurture of life.

Our society, having declared itself free from what might be considered outmoded and Victorian sexual practice, now seems loose on its sexual hinges. Like children set loose without restraint in a candy store, we imagine that we can exercise every sort of freedom without consequences. We find ourselves awash in a world of sexual innuendo and explicitness. Subliminal promises of youth and virility underlie our advertising in every medium. Automobiles are caressed lovingly by lithe maidens while a twentieth-century incarnation of Adonis puts them through their paces. Women are projected as brassy, desiring temptresses, while men are supposed to be dominating jocks. Diet supplements, sprays, mouthwashes, mascaras, and colognes promise to melt away pounds and wrinkles, to set hearts pounding and ensure that we are irresistible. Often, the subliminal image is cast aside, for blatant and crude sexual language and actions are an accepted part of movies and television programs marked for general audiences. There is no protection from the smut that envelops us. While we worry about the pollution of our air and water, which threatens our health and lives, the pollution of our language and images threatens a greater danger. One could wish for a return of at least part of those days when modesty and good taste were a part of life. The prophet Jeremiah speaks twice of those who have become so open minded and so unrestrained in conduct that they have lost their ability to blush. He asks whether they were ashamed when they committed abominations. No, he answers for them, they were not at all ashamed. They did not know how to blush (see Jer. 6:15; 8:12).

> *"Automobiles are caressed lovingly by lithe maidens while a twentieth-century incarnation of Adonis puts them through their paces."*

Who can take any sort of unbiased look at the condition of our society today and not conclude that a people who will not take seriously the intimate and sacred nature of the marriage bed will suffer the conflict, anger, jealousy, guilt, and diseases that are the inevitable result? Most of us are aware that there is a vocal minority in this nation who deny that there are consequences for such actions, but the evidence is too overwhelming to ignore. What makes matters worse is that the guilty do not suffer alone, but the innocent suffer as well. Our recent experiences with AIDS, when it is transmitted to innocent blood recipients and newborn children, are cases in point. We are discovering that what has been foisted upon us in the name of freedom has brought many new bondages.

It is clear that Jesus saw the import, both negative and positive, in his commentary on this command, which makes it even more restrictive: "You have heard that it was said, 'You shall not commit adultery.' But I say to you that everyone who looks at a woman with lust has already committed adultery with her in his heart. If your right eye causes you to sin, tear it out and throw it away; it is better for you to lose one of your members than for your whole body to be thrown into hell" (Matt. 5:27-29).

> *"When the command against adultery is violated, so are all instructions in the last half of the decalogue."*

There are those who think that Jesus was exaggerating or was far too restrictive. Yet one cannot imagine any solution to our present-day problems, unleashed by promiscuity, that would be less direct and demanding. Moreover, Jesus knew what many have understood, that when the command against adultery is violated, so are all instructions in the last half of the decalogue. Relationships are broken (killed), cherished commitments are compromised (stolen), evasions and secretive behavior result (lying). The basic spirit underlying an adulterous liaison is a conviction that in the liaison some real self-fulfillment will be discovered (coveting).

It is tempting to dwell at length on the negative aspects of this commandment and miss the positive matters that it brings to our attention. First, it is important to acknowledge that sexual involvement provides a way for two persons to share the mutuality of their love and to build each other up. No thinking person would play down the matter of sexual passion as a part of who and what we are and hope to be. Those who share the daily responsibilities of home and child care and work are afforded the opportunity to celebrate that sharing through the joy of sex.

Sexuality was given great importance in the practice of circumcision among the Jews. What may have begun as a health measure took on deep religious symbolism among these people. When a man and a woman are engaged in sexual encounter, both can see the mark of circumcision, which is God's mark of ownership of life and a reminder that God is the giver of the power of procreation. Sex, then, was made for joy, and for more. The writers of the Hebrew scriptures do not shy away from noting that God's first command was to have sexual relations—to create (Gen. 1:28). Surely the line about creation in Psalm 8 declares that we are made a little lower than God, who is the Creator. We are privileged to be the instruments of God's will to fill the earth.

It ought to go without saying that this command was given in the interest of community. No community can stay together when there is an easy disregard for the covenant relationship meant to exist between husbands and wives. Jealousies, suspicions, hatreds, and conflict arise in every community where persons take this matter lightly.

Concern for the family lies as much at the heart of this command as it does in the command to keep the sabbath. The family is, as we have noted before, the womb in which life is nourished, the cradle in which character is formed, the crucible where personhood and selfhood are the products of the intense heat generated by people learning how to live with one another and being prepared for life in the larger community.

One cannot deal fairly with the subject of adultery, and especially with Jesus' attitude toward it, without being reminded of the Gospel reports of his encounters with persons identified as sexually unacceptable. Perhaps the fact that both events are reported in the Gospel of John tells us that by the second century such matters could be discussed more readily than earlier on.

In John 4, the story is told of Jesus' encounter at the well with a woman from Samaria. It is shocking enough that a rabbi would talk to a woman in public, but note that since Jesus lets her know that he is aware of her multiple marriages, she is also marked as being guilty of adultery under the strictest interpretation of what he has to say elsewhere. Yet, we do not find him attacking her or passing some judgment on her.

In John 8, the matter is much more explicit. A woman who has been caught in the very act of adultery is brought to Jesus. The law was clear. Those who brought her meant to shower Jesus with the rules. If he let her go without condemnation he was denying that the law of Moses was to be obeyed. If he passed judgment on her he would be admitting that the legalists among them were right. Jesus bent down and wrote something in the sand. Much speculation and debate has failed to unearth what he wrote, but I suggest that he wrote, simply, "Where is the man?" Then he straightened up and challenged her accusers, "Let anyone among you who is without sin be the first to throw a stone at her" (John 8:7*b*). The crowd melted away, and no accusers remained. Jesus refused to join their accusations and shored up what must have become a renewed resolve on the part of the woman by encouraging her to change her ways.

No sermon on adultery ought to be preached without a word about redemption and forgiveness. Who can tell how many in any congregation have hidden from sight some involvement that still rankles and troubles the spirit? In our society the opportunity and the permission for promiscuity lie available on every hand. Men and women are exposed to temptation as never before and many are not prepared to resist that temptation. It is not the task of the church or the minister to drive the stake of hurt deeper but to offer a word of acceptance (not approval) and good news.

It is important to remember that the seventh commandment stands as a sentinel, guarding the God-given gift of procreation, fencing out intruders who would stain a cherished relationship, watching over the sacred task of the home as it offers wholeness to all who live within it.

It is important that we clearly reveal the sordid and callous nature of our society, which claims the right to freedoms that bring hurt and intrude on the freedoms of others. We have a clear call to sensitize our people to a dimension of humanity that expresses itself in what is acceptable and good and perfect. We are a people who once again need to learn to blush.

Above all else, we must extend the word of the gospel and, while withholding judgment, offer redemption and renewal. Then we can lay claim to being disciples of the man who must have been so embarrassed at the plight of the poor woman dragged into his presence that he would not even look at her. I cannot help believing that on that day Jesus blushed.

THE EIGHTH WORD

> *You shall not steal. (Exod. 20:15)*

Hands Off!

Steal what?

These people have been slaves for some time. The opportunity to accumulate wealth and property has not been afforded them. Of course, that does not mean that they have absolutely nothing. In Exodus 5, Moses reminds Pharaoh that when the people leave Egypt, they will want to take their livestock with them. Moses instructs the people to ask their neighbors for "objects of silver and gold" (Exod. 11:2b). By this time the Egyptians are probably ready for them to go, and good riddance. Pharaoh's people have had enough of plagues. A few gold and silver trinkets are minor sacrifices. We know that the Hebrews had quite a bit of gold with them when they left Egypt, since enough was available for Aaron to cast a golden calf for them when Moses was delayed on the mountain. If we prefer to associate this command with return from the exile there is no problem either, since many of those who had been carried off to Babylon had done quite well there. In fact, many of them did not wish to return to Israel.

On the face of this command it is clear that those who flaunt it are those who let loose in the community a spirit of suspicion, hatred, and mistrust that divides and undermines community.

Some persons today grew up in what seemed to them a simpler world. Things like stealing were clearly understood. If you took something from another person, which was clearly that person's property, and intended to keep it, you were stealing. I still feel embarrassment when I remember when my fourth-grade teacher found out that one of the members of the class who was a buddy of mine had stolen a nickel from her desk. She was unrelenting in her punishment. She stood him on her desk and made him apologize for what he had done and then proceeded to drive the lesson home for all of us.

Some members of the Israelite community could well use the warning not to steal. David, who is touted as the ideal model for a king, apparently had a streak of kleptomania. You remember all the lengths to which he went to steal Bathsheba from the unfortunate Uriah. Kings, who had everything, seemed to have a special penchant for things that belonged to others. In I Kings 21 the writer tells the sorry tale of King Ahab's yearning for Naboth's vineyard, which finally encourages Queen Jezebel to hatch a nasty plot against defenseless Naboth that ends in his death and affords Ahab the opportunity to exercise the right of eminent domain and add the vineyard to his other riches.

The prophet Amos unleashes a torrent of accusations at an affluent people whom he claims would steal pennies off the eyes of a dead man. Listen to his vitriolic denouncements:

> Thus says the LORD:
> For three transgressions of Israel,
>   and for four, I will not revoke
>   the punishment;
> because they sell the righteous
>   for silver,
>   and the needy for a pair of sandals. (Amos 2:6)
> Hear this word, you cows of Bashan
>   who are on Mount Samaria,
> who oppress the poor, who
>   crush the needy. (Amos 4:1)

There is abundant accusation in Amos to remind us that it is not always the poor who steal and that there are other ways of stealing than just picking up something that doesn't belong to you.

> *"New ways of stealing: arbitrage, junk bonds, computer hacking, stock manipulation, influence peddling."*

In fact, when we consider what goes on in this nation these days, we see that it seems we have developed stealing into a fine art. So long as there is no law prohibiting excess profiteering, we admire those who can discover the loopholes and make a bundle while everyone is watching. We have added new words to our vocabulary to speak of new ways of stealing: *arbitrage, junk bonds, computer hacking, stock manipulation, influence peddling.*

There are those in our midst who see nothing wrong on the part of those in need if they steal in order to support themselves and their children. Most of the time this is done within the law. When persons refuse to work and exploit all the agencies meant to help the truly needy, not only do they steal from the taxpayers who make funds available, but also they steal from those who are in real need.

State governments have now decided that they can define what kind of stealing can be approved. While officers of the state break up card games at which gamblers seek to make profit at the expense of others, the state itself encourages the hope that one can garner great wealth for a very small investment. State leaders steal from us when they devise lotteries and use every sort of mesmerizing method to entice people to participate and believe that they will not have to pay taxes. The great Savings and Loan debacle of the 1980s and 1990s reveals that those motivated by power and greed have looted the institutions that were once trusted and have stolen not only from depositors and investors, but also from generations of taxpayers who will have to pick up the tab.

> *"State leaders steal from us when they devise lotteries and use every sort of mesmerizing method to entice people to participate and believe that they will not have to pay taxes."*

When people ask for everything from their government and then bring every pressure they can against elected officials to make sure that taxes are kept down, they rob from the future and ensure that their children and grandchildren will not have the largess that has been theirs. There is a great story about this in Nehemiah 5 when the people who have returned from exile in Babylon find themselves strapped by high taxes and inflation and cry out their resentment: "Now our flesh is the same as that of our kindred; our children are the same as their children; and yet we are forcing our sons and daughters to be slaves, and some of our daughters have been ravished; we are powerless, and our fields and vineyards now belong to others" (Neh. 5:5).

We steal from the future if we seek to have everything we want and do not pay the price. In a very special way we have opportunity to steal from one another and without the finger of accusation pointing at us, as did Ahab.

When, in an effort to lower taxes, we lobby against funds for education and programs designed to break the cycle of poverty, we steal from those who are doomed to empty lives in ghettos across the nation.

When we take the gift of dominion to mean that we can exploit and rule our environment for profit, we steal health and life and joy from all those who are made bereft of a world that is whole. All of us are victims—those who steal and those who are stolen from—when the quality of life for all is brought low because of our profligate ways.

74

Even in the church the matter of theft must be considered. Of course, few of us would be prone to carry off anything from the church. But the prophet Malachi raises an issue that strikes home for many: "Will anyone rob God? Yet you are robbing me! But you say, "How are we robbing you?" In your tithes and offerings! You are cursed with a curse, for you are robbing me—the whole nation of you!" (Mal. 3:8-9).

This accusation could raise some interesting questions for many of us. How many of us have nice boats or swimming pools or fancy automobiles? Would we admit that we stole them? Of course not. We have the checks and the receipts. But with whose money were they purchased? Who went uncared for because of these things? A tough word, but one that needs to be heard.

The prophet Haggai brings God's word to the leaders of Judah who have been stalling in the rebuilding of the Temple. He declares:

> These people say the time has not yet come to rebuild the LORD's house. . . . Is it a time for you yourselves to live in your paneled houses, while this house lies in ruins? Now therefore thus says the LORD of hosts: Consider how you have fared. You have sown much, and harvested little; you eat, but you never have enough; you drink, but you never have your fill; you clothe yourselves, but no one is warm; and you that earn wages earn wages to put them into a bag with holes. (Hag. 1:2-6)

Can anyone find a better description of a people who are affluent, and yet seem never to be satisfied? Is there something about our attitude that allows us to steal and not be aware of it? Even more, to think that what we do is all right? Are we blind to our own subtle and so common taking from others that it has never occurred to us that we are thieves?

"Many employees have never imagined that they were stealing."

75

We read much about white-collar crime these days, that petty thievery by which little things disappear from the office. Pencils, paper, stationery, supplies of every kind are easy to hide and carry away. So difficult has the problem become that employers use lie detectors to check the honesty of their employees. So rampant is the problem that many employees have never imagined that they were stealing, but consider what they took as a fringe benefit.

What is bad for many is plain stealing of another's property. We are in general agreement that when people do such things they ought to be punished.

What is worse is the state of mind and heart on the part of many who do not even imagine that they steal from others when they dodge taxes or engage in conspicuous consumption or are profligate with the God-given gifts of the earth.

But worst of all is to steal from God.

God has laid claim on our lives, our energies, our talents, and our treasures. We are given dominion, responsibility for all these things and for one another. When we violate that trust we steal from one another, from ourselves, and from God. If we listen carefully we might again hear the prophet warning us to keep our hands off what God calls his own.

THE NINTH WORD

> *You shall not bear false witness against your neighbor. (Exod. 20:16)*

Who Can You Trust?

This commandment is not meant exclusively for the new community to be established by the returned slaves recently freed from bondage in Egypt or for the group led back home by Ezra and Nehemiah following the Babylonian Exile. Even in the wilderness of the exodus and exile to Babylon there was a need for persons to be able to trust one another's word. There would be inevitable counter claims, disputes over incidents, and accusations that required some adjudication.

Sometimes the matter may have been brought before those responsible for settling such disputes. Remember that just before Israel came to Sinai, Moses had been acting as sole judge for all occasions. Jethro, Moses' father-in-law, points out that Moses is wearing himself out trying to be all things to all people, and that he should choose men to care for such matters so he can be free for more important tasks (see Exod. 18). Property, reputations, even lives could be at stake. The matter became especially serious if one was accused of a breach of the law. Words could wound and destroy. They could undermine the foundations of any sense of community that could have existed even in the wilderness.

The failure of handling the truth lightly had been dealt with already in the story of the Garden of Eden. It is generally thought that this and other stories in Genesis were put into writing by the priests in the fifth century BCE or so, but that does not mean that they had their beginning then. Such stories had to have some ancient roots, and many of them clearly do. In Genesis 3 the serpent says to Eve what she and every one of us since want to hear: "You will not die." The serpent tells her that God is lying. God is jealous and doesn't want her to know what the gods know and become like them. That big lie had its effect, and it continues to have its effect and cause great mischief.

The story of the New Testament church begins with the same kind of problem. Everybody agrees to share possessions in common so that all would have what they needed. However, Ananias and Sapphira sell their property and keep back some of the proceeds for themselves. In effect, they lie about what they have to share. Their deaths must have made a considerable impression on that early community (see Acts 5).

Everywhere in the scriptures the right handling of the truth is held important. In Psalm 27 the poet asks to be protected from false witnesses. Who can forget the sin of Achan, who keeps a part of the spoils from the battle at Ai and brings about the death of his entire family (Josh. 7:24-26)? Dealing falsely did not always mean dealing with words.

The New Testament is filled with concern for the truth as well. Jesus has his say in the Sermon on the Mount:

> You have heard that it was said to those of ancient times, "You shall not swear falsely, but carry out the vows you have made to the Lord." But I say to you, Do not swear at all, either by heaven, for it is the throne of God, or by the earth, for it is his footstool, or by Jerusalem, for it is the city of the great King. And do not swear by your head, for you cannot make one hair white or black. Let your word be "Yes, Yes" or "No, No"; anything more than this comes from the evil one. (Matt. 5:33-37)

> ## *"Plain and clear talk is best of all."*

The writer of the letter to Ephesus counsels that all speak the truth with their neighbor (Eph. 4:25). Paul commands the Colossians not to lie to one another (Col. 3:9). James makes extensive comment on the dangers that lie with the tongue (James 3:1-12). Each echoes the words of Jesus, who clears away all the ifs, ands, buts, and whereases in the Sermon on the

Mount, saying, "Let your word be 'Yes, Yes' or 'No, No'" (Matt. 5:37). Clearly he is referring to the taking of oaths in the legal sense. In other words, plain and clear talk is best of all.

Who would deny that we live in a world that needs to hear someone express concern for the truth? We have become too accustomed to propaganda that twists the truth to serve some political purpose. Many have grown openly cynical to campaign promises to the point that few take political platforms seriously anymore. We have watched as accused persons have appealed to the fifth amendment in order to avoid revealing their lawbreaking behavior. We have become painfully aware of erased tapes, doctored evidence, and illegal cover-ups. There are those who envy others who can twist the truth to their advantage and avoid responsibilities. Lawyers become famous for their abilities to take sharp advantage of the law. We speak of doublespeak, words that make lies sound like the truth, and credibility gaps. Resumes are padded with non-existent accomplishments. Perjury has become all too familiar.

Advertisers are expected to exaggerate and misrepresent products. Some people who would not think of telling a lie are able to keep silent when trading a lemon automobile in on a better deal.

The list hardly requires the addition of further illustrations. We have become a people who take the matter of telling the truth lightly and are the worse for it. It is not only the individual who needs to hear a word of warning, but also political parties that make promises they do not intend to keep, corporate officials who misrepresent their products or their financial condition, nations that deal in deception with other nations—all these need to hear the word that such mishandling of the truth is at the base of much of the distrust, inability to negotiate, stress, and conflict that is abroad in the world these days.

By our use of the language, we have created a world in which differing people mean differing things by the same words, (peace, war, wealth, nationalism, hostage), and Babel is present once again.

> *"We can, if we wish, use the truth to hurt and wound."*

Some, no doubt, wonder whether it is being suggested that we tell the truth at all costs and no matter what. Sooner or later every discussion of the ninth commandment comes to the issue of what are called the finer points of consideration. It seems clear to me that we can, if we wish, use the truth to hurt and to wound. When the truth is revealed out of a sense of malice, hate, and envy, then the truth, meant for the good, becomes a weapon for doing evil. When the writer of the letter to Ephesus speaks about truth telling he makes a critical point: "So then, putting away falsehood, let all of us speak the truth to our neighbors, for we are members of one another" (Eph. 4:25).

That is the point! We are members of one another. We live in a common bundle. We share a relationship of solidarity. We carry within us the capacity to help or to hurt.

It is not the purpose of this commentary to deal with every question that could be raised and leave nothing uncovered. It is enough for us to maintain that one of the requirements of community is truth telling. This is something more than just not being false. It calls for us to be fully aware of the hurt we can inflict and to take great pains to avoid such actions.

All of us are aware that we live in a broken world and that not everything will always appear simple. Even so, we are not to take that as a reason for dealing loosely with the truth. We are still under command to let our yes be yes and our no be no, and to remember that we are members one of another. There is no escaping that.

THE TENTH WORD

You shall not covet your neighbor's house; you shall not covet your neighbor's wife, or male or female slave, or ox, or donkey, or anything that belongs to your neighbor. (Exod. 20:17)

A Matter of the Heart

At first glance we may wonder why there is a commandment on stealing and another on coveting. They seem to cover much of the same territory. For example, while Jesus did comment on four of the last five commandments, he is not recorded as having specifically commented on the eighth.

On the face of the matter it seems enough to say that coveting leads to stealing, and we can hardly argue with that. But if we dig a bit deeper we begin to see that at least on another level the eighth commandment seems to have to do with property and possessions, while the tenth has to do with family and living things. Even then, however, there is a deeper level on which the difference can be better exposed.

Stealing seems better linked to clear and simple selfishness. Someone has something that we want to have for ourselves, and so we reach out and take it. Covetousness, however, seems to have more to do with an attitude deep within, a spirit that reveals something of the basis on which we build life.

I suspect that many understand the command against coveting to mean that they are not to want what others have. They are to take a vow of poverty and take no thought for tomorrow. I find no command that requires that we not be prudent about life, that we make no preparation for the future. What else can be the meaning of stories told by Jesus about the person who built a house on sand (Matt. 7:24-27) or about the person who built a tower without assurance of sufficient resources (Luke 14:28-33)? We are expected to use our good sense and make proper provision for life.

> *"Coveting is . . . a conviction that what we can possess brings real meaning into life."*

Coveting is a matter of the heart, a spirit, a conviction that what we can possess brings real meaning into life. Jesus gave us the clearest definition of coveting in his encounter with the rich fool, as reported in Luke 12:13-21. A man steps out of the crowd that had come to hear Jesus, and, apparently judging Jesus to be a man of both good sense and an honest spirit, asks Jesus to tell his brother (apparently the firstborn) to divide the family inheritance with him. I have often wondered whether this is a second chapter of the story of the prodigal son. Remember, it is this son who squandered what his father had given him, much of which really belonged to the elder brother. Does he want even more now that the father is dead? Jesus' answer strikes at the heart of covetousness: "Friend, who set me to be a judge or arbitrator over you?" (Luke 12:14). Then Jesus speaks to the crowd: "Take care! Be on your guard against all kinds of greed [the RSV uses the word *covetousness*]; for one's life does not consist in the abundance of possessions" (Luke 12:15).

Jesus follows with the story of the rich man who has a bumper crop of grain and wonders what to do with it. He decides to build new and larger barns in which to store his excess so that he will never have to worry about tomorrow.

Covetousness is the spirit that bases life's security on the things we can gather together. Storing up riches, harboring more than we need, and excessive accumulation of things betrays a spirit of not trusting God for life. Jesus has put his finger on the problem.

Coveting goes beyond desire; it even goes beyond stealing. It has to do with obtaining things legitimately and trusting in them to give life meaning. Coveting can be rooted in many things: pride, anxiety, seeking power, ostentatiousness—you name it. Few of us would have any trouble identifying covetousness these days. On every hand we are bombarded by subliminal advertising messages that promise all the things we want most: sexual virility, painless living, and the dream of immortality. These messages are meant not just to get us to want things but to make us believe that we cannot live without them. We become so anxious that we are ready to take whatever action and risks that are necessary in order to gain the thing we covet.

It is little wonder that Jesus gives so much attention to this greedy spirit in the Sermon on the Mount. Following the commentary on the hoarding of earthly treasures (Matt. 6:19-21), the need for the healthy eye (Matt. 6:22-23), and a reminder that no one can successfully serve two masters (Matt. 6:24), he continues: "Therefore I tell you, do not worry about your life, what you will eat or what you will drink, or about your body, what you will wear. Is not life more than food, and the body more than clothing?" (Matt. 6:25). The modern advertising industry would answer with a resounding no.

The point is that too many of us take the short view of life and have fallen victim to the often repeated phrase "You only go around once, so grab all the gusto you can." It is the lack of belief in life lived in the context of eternity that leads to covetousness. It is little wonder, then, that Jesus recommends flowers and birds as models. They do what they are supposed to do, and so should we. Just as they are made to flourish for a while and disappear, so also we are made for eternity and cannot find true life until we accept that as true. So it is commanded—or, to put it another way, it is mandatory—that we "strive first for the kingdom of God and his righteousness, and all these things will be given to you as well" (Matt. 6:33).

To strive for the kingdom is to strive for a view of life that knows that the present and eternity are in God's hand. To seek God's righteousness rather than our own is to admit that whatever righteousness we have is a gift, and that we have it because God gives it, because we are accepted as righteous even when we are imperfect.

In the RSV, the healthy eye is the sound eye; in the KJV it is the single eye. I like the word *single* because it stands in contrast to the double heart pictured in Matthew 6:24. It is a fact of life. We cannot be loyal to two masters. The people of Israel tried it. The writer of II Kings tells us that the Israelites "worshiped the LORD but also served their own gods" (II Kings 17:33*a*).

One of the problems present-day Christians have is that many of us see no connection between belief and life. We go to church regularly, make a pledge and pay it, serve on committees, and are in general great church persons. But then from day to day we listen to the siren songs of the media, fall victim to the enchantments of the baubles life has to offer, become convinced that it doesn't matter how a thing is obtained or whether it makes sense, but it must be gotten because, in the words of a TV advertisement, "I'm worth it." Such a spirit lies close to the heart of covetousness.

To be convinced that the meaning of life has to do with possessions, to take the short view of life and miss the eternal context in which we live, to seek to serve all the gods—all this is at the root of covetousness.

But what about those times when we speak of coveting good things? Is that all right?

> *"Jesus knew the difference between trust and lust."*

It is if we keep our definitions in mind. If we truly believe that the good things are meant to enhance life, if what we covet are those things that have to do with eternity (treasures in heaven; Matt. 5:20), if we earnestly strive for the greater gifts as Paul advises in I Corinthians 12:31, then we are coveting in the best sense.

But does this really mean that we cannot want anything, that it is wrong for us to desire good food, excellent clothes, a nice house or car? Surely it does not mean this if we are speaking of wanting or needing or desiring. Coveting takes another step and concludes that selfhood and meaning can be had only if we possess something. There is no command in the Bible that requires us to be poverty stricken. Jesus did not condemn wealth. He did warn about wealth, since he knew that the line between wanting and coveting is a thin line and is easily crossed after a bit of self-delusion. Jesus knew the difference between trust and lust.

Trust is that spirit that accepts life as a gift from the hand of God, embraces the idea that life should be lived fruitfully for oneself and for others, and does not let anxiety eat at the roots of faith and drive us to seek to worship all the gods. Trust is based on the conviction that this world was created by God (see Genesis 1) and that God cares for all his creation in the present.

Lust is present when we are overwhelmed and driven by self-concern and the short view of life. Like the rich fool, we look forward to the day when we can eat, drink, and be merry while we can, for tomorrow we may die. That spirit still lives among some of us who live fruitful and sharing lives and then at retirement retreat from the world and its concerns and let anxiety for tomorrow drive our decisions. That spirit still lives among the young who must have all the outer symbols offered by the world in order to have identity, unaware that they are driven to such measures because they have no solid self-image and do not know who they are. That spirit still lives among the middle aged who have failed to reach all their goals and begin to retreat into a safe world where there are no uncertainties and thereby abandon their responsibility to take risks on behalf of the world just when they are most prepared to be involved.

> *"Coveting always involves the worship of some short-term promise (idolatry)."*

Coveting is much like adultery. It is difficult to keep a definition of it from spilling over into other areas. Coveting can lead to falsifying records, creating false impressions (lying). It can lead to obtaining what we covet by unscrupulous methods (stealing). Coveting always involves the worship of some short-term promise (idolatry). It can cause us to look at another person's spouse lustfully (adultery).

Coveting can bring every sort of mischief into the community and tear at the fabric of the relationships that are meant to hold the community together. Everybody knows the person who is on the make, who is always ready to benefit at cost to others, who puts self before anything or anyone else, who lives as though today is all there is, who gathers and gathers and yet seems never to be quite satisfied, never quite fulfilled.

At the heart of coveting is the lack of a clear self-image, and this drives us to keep accumulating outer representations, outer symbols that are meant to tell others who and what we are. Strip away all those symbols, take away all the props by which we convince ourselves and others that we are somebody, and disaster comes. Nothing remains but an empty shell. Jesus' words ring with more relevance in this world of ours than many of us have imagined: "Take care! Be on your guard against all kinds of greed; for one's life does not consist in the abundance of possessions" (Luke 12:15).

The Last Word

When I was in the fourth grade our new teacher made a valiant attempt to convince all of us that cleanliness was next to godliness. Somewhere she found samples of a soap and an accompanying chart on which there were ten checkpoints for daily cleanliness. Every day school began with a Bible reading, a prayer, and then health inspection. Two students served as the weekly doctor and nurse. They put on their doctor and nurse hats and then went up and down the aisles, checking each of us for (1) clean hands, (2) clean teeth, (3) combed hair, (4) clean ears, (5) clean clothes, (6) clean socks, (7) polished shoes, (8) a clean handkerchief, (9) a pocket comb, and (10) clean fingernails. If you made it on all ten points, you got a gold star on the chart provided by the soap company. If you failed at any point, your name was dutifully inscribed in large letters in a "mud hole" that was prominently drawn on the chalkboard. There your name stayed until you cleaned up your act.

When I listen to people discussing the Ten Commandments, I am convinced that this is the way many understand them. Keep all ten and get a gold star for the heavenly crown. Miss one, and you are in the mud hole.

In the introduction, I mentioned the 3-by-6-foot chart on the wall of my home church. It hung there week after week as a reminder of our goals, rules to be kept, and standards to be maintained. The implication was that we could go to church on Sunday, and scan down the list and breathe a sigh of relief at getting through another week with no violations, and then hope that somewhere up there in heaven some administrative angel was licking a gold star for our chart.

It is important that we pause again and recall the context in which the Exodus account of the giving of the Ten Commandments, which are more accurately called the Ten Words, is set. Remember, this is a band of people recently freed from Egyptian slavery, standing at Mount Sinai, midway between 430 years of bondage in Egypt and the call to a new destiny of nationhood in a new land. Our thesis has been that what is recorded here are not ten moral commands for everyone to keep circumspectly in order to be blessed, but that they are ten words addressing four themes basic to the formation of community.

We are not the first to take the wrong track. Mark tells of one who came to Jesus and asked, "Good Teacher, what must I do to inherit eternal life?" (Mark 10:17). Jesus replies with a list of some of the commands: "You know the commandments: 'Do not kill. Do not commit adultery. Do not steal. Do not bear false witness. Do not defraud. Honor your father and mother" (Mark 10:18-19, paraphrased).

The man responds: "Teacher, I have kept all these since my youth" (Mark 10:20). You can hear his meaning: "I have checked off the commands one by one. I have been examined. My ears are clean. I have my comb and handkerchief; my chart is filled with gold stars. My name is not in the mud hole."

Mark tells us that Jesus loved him, and then gave him a new command that was just for him. He was to sell what he owned and give the proceeds to the poor. Jesus knew what stood between the young man and eternal life.

For Jesus, and I think the writer of Exodus, something more was at stake than observing rules. The spirit, the attitude, and the heart that underlie all actions are more important than the actions themselves. Surely that is what Jesus had in mind when he prefaced his commentary on the commands by saying: "Do not think that I have come to abolish the law or the prophets; I have come not to abolish but to fulfill. . . . I tell you, unless your righteousness exceeds that of the scribes and Pharisees, you will never enter the kingdom of heaven" (Matt. 5:17, 20).

Exceeds the righteousness of those who made a career and lifetime of seeking to observe all the commands?

It is clear that Jesus was concerned for something more than the scrupulous and meticulous keeping of every detail of the law. Matthew spreads that concern before us in the Sermon on the Mount as he quotes Jesus' famous "You have heard," "But I say" passages. It is clear that Jesus digs much deeper than rule keeping and shows a concern for the spirit that is behind the act. I am convinced that Matthew considers this matter of great importance since he writes to a church that is in intense dialogue with the scribes and Pharisees over the finer points related to gaining God's approval.

Jesus is repeatedly portrayed as keeping his concern for the inner motive, the bent of the spirit, the intent of the heart. In Matthew 22:34-40 we read of the time when a lawyer (one of the scribes, expert in the law), comes to test Jesus, asking, "Teacher, which commandment in the law is the greatest?" (Matt. 22:36). Jesus replies: " 'You shall love the Lord your God with all your heart, and with all your soul, and with all your mind.' This is the greatest and first commandment. And a second is like it: 'You shall love your neighbor as yourself" (Matt. 22:37-39).

Jesus links two scriptures, Deuteronomy 8:5 and Leviticus 19:18, to spell out the basic commitment of any person who means to keep the spirit and the letter of the law. In Matthew 15, Jesus follows an encounter with the legalists with a commentary on things that are defiling. He concludes: "What comes out of the mouth proceeds from the heart, and this is what defiles. For out of the heart come evil intentions, murder, adultery, fornication, theft, false witness, slander" (Matt. 15:18-19).

It is clear that Jesus had problems making his point about the heart and spirit with the religious legalists in his day and that the church continued to face that problem in the first century, since all the synoptics have something to say at this point.

There were those who arrived at an opposite conclusion. Since grace abounded, and since all was forgiven by a loving God, there was nothing to worry about. One could forget rules and regulations.

Paul had to deal with this problem at Rome. In his often-used form of diatribe he summarizes the position of his opponents: "Should we continue in sin in order that grace may abound?" (Rom. 6:1). There were those who imagined that since grace came into play every time someone sinned and repented the thing to do was to sin much so there would be much grace.

Paul replies, "God forbid!" He cannot believe his ears. How can those who have been redeemed think such things? For him the new life is a response to the gift of grace, and no one should take that gift lightly.

In Romans 7, Paul maintains that to present grace does not mean that the law has no purpose. He writes: "What then should we say? That the law is sin? By no means! Yet, if it had not been for the law, I would not have known sin" (Rom. 7:7). For Paul the law performs the function of teaching us how to respond to grace. The law instructs us and enables us to avoid the pitfalls of sin.

Though there were those who thought otherwise, Jesus never took the commands lightly. His comment on the command concerning adultery in Matthew 5:29 says much about his concern: "If your right eye causes you to sin, tear it out and throw it away; it is better for you to lose one of your members than for your whole body to be thrown into hell."

This and his comment to the same effect concerning an offending right hand say something about Jesus' deep concern for right living whether we say we are to take him literally or not.

When we consider the matter of concern for morality and ethics from the standpoint of watching the church struggle with the issue from Paul to Mark to Matthew to Luke, it is clear that the church did not relent and finally won the day from both the legalists and those who sought license.

The evidence that the church finally made its point can be found in the Gospel of John as Jesus talks with his disciples just before taking leave of them. He says, "I give you a new commandment, that you love one another. Just as I have loved you, you also should love one another. By this everyone will know that you are my disciples, if you have love for one another" (John 13:34-35).

When we add this expansion of the command for us to love our neighbor to Jesus' summarizing of the first three commandments in the decalogue with the command to love God with heart and mind and soul and strength, it is clear that Jesus was concerned both for the letter and for the spirit of the law. Both were important when the new community was about to come into being after the bondage of Egypt, when a new community was to be constructed following the Babylonian Exile, and when a new community was called into being by Jesus' life and death and resurrection. These commandments, these ten words, served then and now as an explication of the four bases on which community can be established and can endure.

Our conclusion is clear. Our righteousness must exceed a concern for keeping the rules, working for stars, and avoiding mud holes. Our righteousness has to do with obedience to God's will as made it known to us, with the heart, the spirit, the attitude, and the commitment that are within us. If any people are to find unity, to become a community in which life can have meaning and endurance, to find eternal life, then it will be a people who clearly understands the four messages in these ten words. We are to be a community:

1. Whose loyalty and obedience and worship are to one God (Commandments 1, 2, and 3).

2. Whose concern is for the worth and value of every individual (Commandment 4).

3. Whose support is given to the health and coherence of the family (Commandment 5).

4. That encourages a spirit in which there is regard for persons and property, and that makes for peace and wholeness (Commandments 6-10).

These are not ten simple rules that God gives us to follow so that God can love us and reward us with eternal life so much as they are a design for response to God's call for obedience and the formation of community. Here are reminders of what must exist in a nation if that nation is to endure.

In my fourth-grade class, most of us were clean, not because we thought being clean was important. We just didn't want our names to be written in the mud hole. We wanted the stars.

Jesus knew that our fascination for winning stars by keeping the rules is usually tainted by self-concern. He also knew that we ought to have a greater concern than just winning heaven or escaping hell. The clue to his teaching is given in his commentary on the last command: "Strive first for the kingdom of God and his righteousness, and all these things will be given to you as well" (Matt. 6:33).

An anonymous poet put it in proper words long ago:

> My God, I love thee not because
> I hope for heaven thereby,
> Nor yet because, if I love not,
> I must forever die.
> Thou, O my Jesus, thou didst me
> Upon the cross embrace;
> For me didst bear the nails and spear,
> And manifold disgrace.
> Then why, O blessed Jesus Christ,
> Should I not love thee well?
> Not for the sake of winning heaven,
> Nor of escaping hell.
> Not with the hope of gaining aught,
> Not seeking a reward,
> But as thyself has loved me,
> O everloving Lord.
> So would I love thee, dearest Lord,
> And in thy praise will sing;
> Because thou art my loving God,
> and my eternal King.

Suggested Reading

Barclay, William. *Matthew,* The Daily Bible Study Series. Philadelphia: Westminster Press, 1958.

———. *The Ten Commandments for Today.* New York: Harper & Row, 1973.

Calvin, John. *Sermons on the Ten Commandments.* Grand Rapids: Baker, 1980.

Eliot, T. S. *The Complete Poems and Plays.* New York: Harcourt, Brace and World, 1972.

Harrelson, Walter. *The Ten Commandments and Human Rights.* Philadelphia: Fortress Press, 1980.

"The Decalogue." *Interpretation* 43, 3 (July 1989).

Mould, Elmer W. K. *Essentials of Bible History.* rev. ed. New York: The Ronald Press, 1951.

The United Methodist Hymnal. Nashville: The United Methodist Publishing House, 1989.